M000313736

Game On!
Change is
Constant

Tactics to Win When Leading Change is
Everyone's Business

KAREN FERRIS

Game On! Change is Constant

Copyright © Karen Ferris 2018

Typeset by BookPOD

Disclaimer
The material in this book is general comment only and neither purports nor intends to be specific advice related to any particular reader. It does not represent professional advice and should not be relied on as the basis for any decision or action on any matter that it covers. To the maximum extent permitted by law, the author and publisher disclaim all responsibility and liability to any person or entity, whether a purchaser or not, in respect to anything and of the consequences of anything done by any such person in reliance, whether in whole or in part, upon the whole or any part of the contents of this publication.

ISBN: 978-0-6484694-0-7 (pbk)

 A catalogue record for this book is available from the National Library of Australia

About the author

Karen Ferris is an unashamed organizational change management rebel with a cause. She likes to challenge the status quo but only when her reason for doing so is defensible.

Karen began her working life in IT but has spent a large part of her career in the IT service management space where she is recognized globally for her expertise and insight.

As someone continually focused on the people side of change, Karen authored a publication entitled *Balanced Diversity: A Portfolio Approach to Organizational Change* back in 2010. She considered herself an accidental author back then. She stumbled across a framework for embedding change, set out to write a whitepaper about it and ended up with a book on her hands. That was the moment where she was propelled into the world of organizational change management.

Karen is a sought after international keynote speaker, coach, mentor, facilitator, and trainer.

Born in Liverpool, UK, she immigrated to Australia in 1998. She lives with her wife, Breed, in Melbourne. She is an avid Liverpool Football Club supporter, an Elvis fan, has an obsession for shoes, and is a self-confessed arctophile—you might want to Google that.

Contents

Introduction

It is game day. Your team is playing a big match in the competition. The opposition is strong, skillful, fit, and fast. It's going to be a tough one to win.

The sound of rattling turnstiles fills the air. You take your seat and absorb the excitement around you. The crowd is growing, and the anticipation is building. Your team enters the ground to a tumultuous roar of support.

This game, as with every game, is different to the last. The ground conditions, the weather, and the opposition have all changed. As a result, the game tactics, team composition, and player positions have changed in order to win the game.

Your team is fast, agile, and quick to fill the open spaces. The players are collaborating, being innovative and creative, and are adapting as the opposition tries to get ahead. Your team is dominating the game, and the opposing players don't know what has hit them.

Your team wins in a decisive manner. The way in which they are playing means they are unrivaled, unequaled, and incomparable with other teams.

You ponder. *How awesome would it be if my organization operated like my winning team? What does my team have that my organization doesn't?*

The answer is resilience. Your team players adapt to ever changing conditions with resilience. Constant change is their norm. They don't resist it. They say 'bring it on,' and get on with the job at hand.

Organizations can echo the traits of winning sports teams and stay ahead of the game. Change is increasingly disruptive, constant, complex, uncertain, and is happening at speeds never known before. If organizations are to win in this volatile environment, they need to be resilient in the face of constant change.

ॐ

This book will introduce the tactics needed by organizations to be resilient and successful. These tactics will enable your organization to triumph in the face of adversity.

I will continue to use a sporting analogy throughout the book. Actually, to be more precise, I will use a soccer analogy. I am from Liverpool in the UK, and I am staunch Liverpool Football Club Supporter. If soccer is not your thing, you can relate the analogy to any team field sport. It could be rugby, cricket, basketball, netball, Australian rules, hurling, hockey, softball, baseball, volleyball, lacrosse, and so on.

It doesn't matter what game your team is playing. The key is that they are fit, skilled, capable, supported, and well-prepared for constant change.

It's *game on*, so let's get training.

PART 1

CHANGE IS CONSTANT

CHAPTER 1

Constant change is the new black

Soccer players today have to be fitter, quicker, and cover more ground in order to beat the competition. Advances and innovations in technology such as boots, strip, kit, balls, fields, goal line technology, and video refereeing are making the game increasingly competitive. Teams have to stay ahead of the game and embrace the constant disruption of technology while responding to constant changes in the competition and conditions.

Organizations face the same challenges. Change is now constant.

Organizational change management, as an approach, needs to undergo radical transformation if it is to be of any value when constant change is the new black. Organizational change management practitioners will have to change their thinking and approach to be relevant.

I have done considerable work examining what I think are the changes needed within organizations where change is constant. I am looking at these from an organizational change management perspective—the people side of change.

Disruption

We hear a lot about *digital disruption* and *digital transformation*. Digital transformation is nothing new. The first computers were introduced in the 1930s but we have been finding faster and more automated ways of doing things long before that. The dishwasher was invented in 1886, and the first electric vacuum cleaner was introduced in 1901.

I don't think it is so much about digital transformation but more so the disruption we are feeling today as change gets faster, and less predictable and manageable.

Organizations that will survive and thrive amidst the disruption are those that truly accept that change is now constant. They will be organizations that embrace the ever-increasing changes in volatility, uncertainly, complexity, and ambiguity (VUCA).

VUCA is not a new term. It was coined in the 1990s by the US Military to describe conditions resulting from the Cold War. It's now used widely in the business world to describe the terrain in which we operate:

- Volatile: constant and significant change
- Uncertain: events and outcomes are unpredictable
- Complex: many interconnected parts and variables
- Ambiguous: a lack of clarity, no precedents, the unknown unknowns

The old approaches to change no longer work

Psychologist Kurt Lewin has long been attributed with the organizational change management model, *Change as Three Steps* (CATS): unfreeze, transition, refreeze.

This model, quoted as being included first in the 1947 journal *Human Relations,* in fact, does not exist.

Yet it is has become a myth that forms the foundation for so many organizational change management approaches and one that has been referenced extensively in organizational change management material.

A Google search for *Lewin freeze* returned 335,000 results on 23/07/2018—not bad for a person who never said it. So despite Lewin being misattributed with the CATS framework, I have to use the framework which has formed the cornerstone of so many organizational change frameworks and approaches, to explain why they no longer work in an environment of constant, volatile and relentless change.

The framework describes the three phases as unfreeze: prepare for change; transition: change and move toward a new way of being; and refreeze: establishing stability once the change has been made.

But today, there is no stability.

William Bridges, the renowned organizational consultant, has a transition model also with three phases: ending, losing, letting go; the neutral zone; and the new beginning that is comparable to that of Lewin's model.

Other approaches operate in cadence with Lewin and Bridges.

The Accelerated Implementation Methodology® (AIM) from IMA has a three-phase process: plan, implement, and monitor.[1] Prosci®, one of the most widely used approaches to organizational change today, also has a three-phase process: prepare for change, manage change, and reinforce change.[2]

We are living in a world that will require a different approach to change and transition. We are not in a state where we can plan, do, embed, and then wait for the next change. Rinse and repeat! Those days are gone. Constant change is the new black.

A different approach

Today, transitioning people through change is continual and multi-faceted. We are no longer in a situation where change happens every so often and disrupts what we were doing. It is driven from the top and cascades through a hierarchical chain of command.

Today's organizational world is one in which everyone can initiate change, everyone can experiment, and everyone is allowed to fail. Everyone has the capability and permission to be self-organizing so that change can be truly constant. Energy and ideas come from the entire organization.

Change is constant

Constant change is the new norm. To thrive in this changing world, organizations have to enable employees to *continually* transition to different ways of working. We do not have the capacity to 'manage' people through such phases of transition in today's VUCA world.

In this book, I will explore how organizations and the people within them need to transform to become the organization that says *we're always ready—game on.*

The succeeding chapters will explore each of these areas in detail:

- People transitions
- Kill the hierarchy
- Let go
- Permission
- Give it up
- Adaptive leadership
- Adaptive leadership teams
- The need for speed.

The following is an overview of each of those areas.

People transitions

We have to recognize that transitioning people through change is now continual and multi-faceted. We must have an agile, iterative approach to organizational change while remaining cognizant of people's needs and individual journeys.

When you look at the 'traditional' organizational change management approaches widely used today, there are a myriad of roles to be played. Sponsors, executive sponsors, supporting sponsors, stakeholders, change agents, change champions, change targets, change consultants, change analysts, and so on.

In our *brave new world,* we don't have time to ensure all these roles are in place and ready for the next change, and that people have the right skills and capabilities to fulfill these roles. We have to keep things simple so that they are *agile*. In the same light, we do not have time to create comprehensive change plans covering sponsorship, coaching, communication, training, resistance management, and reinforcement. Those days are gone.

The only roles we need when we have a sound base for relentless change are managers, coaches, and players. In a nutshell, these roles are:

* **Managers** who determine the strategy that is going to be played out and direct the gameplay.
* **Coaches** ensure that players are game fit.
* **Players** are ultimately those who will win or lose the game.

Kill the hierarchy

While acknowledging that leadership is important, we need a collaborative workplace in which transparency and creative freedom reign over hierarchical boundaries. In order to respond to constant change, we need to be innovative, agile, enable rapid decision-making, and ensure employee engagement.

The organization needs to move from hierarchical 'control' to a flatter structure. It's not about having no structure but using the job of hierarchy to get rid of the bad bureaucracy. Flat organizations are not flat; they are just flatter than tall organizations. Instead of 'shifting the responsibility' up the management ladder, flat structures empower employees to take charge, help make decisions, and feel responsible for the company's success.

A flatter structure facilitates a greater level of communication between employees and management. These organizations are more democratic and offer a greater level of innovation. Communication is faster, more reliable, and more effective than in tall structures. Direct staff input leads to more support for decisions and fewer behind-the-scenes power struggles and disagreements. These organizations can respond to constant change.

The winning soccer team thrives on collaboration, innovation, agility, and delegated decision-making. Managers, coaches, and players all contribute to the gameplay. The players make decisions on the fly depending on what is happening on the field. They may take direction from the managers and the coaches but they don't have to wait until half time to present an idea and wait for it to be sanctioned. By that time, the game is lost.

Shining examples

One organization that didn't need to flatten its structure was W.L. Gore, one of the most successful organizations in the world today. Gore has more than 10,000 employees and three levels of hierarchy. The CEO is elected democratically; there is a handful of functional managers, and then there is everyone else. Decision-making is delegated to self-managing teams of 8–12 people.

Former Gore CEO Terri Kelly said:

'It's far better to rely upon a broad base of individuals and leaders who share a common set of values and feel personal ownership for the overall success of the organization. These responsible and empowered individuals will serve as much better watchdogs than any single, dominant leader or bureaucratic structure.'[3]

One of the most prominent and successful computer game makers is Valve. Valve's employee handbook says:

'Nobody 'reports to' anybody. Nobody 'reports to' anybody else. We do have a founder/president, but even he isn't your manager. This company is yours to steer – toward opportunities and away from risks'.[4]

At Semco, the Brazilian conglomerate, decision-making is delegated. When Ricardo Semler joined the organization as chairman in 1983, he worked tirelessly to distribute decision-making. Now, one of the firm's key performance indicators is how long Semler can go between making decisions. The time keeps getting longer, while the firm has maintained around 20% growth for nearly 30 years now.

Under Semler's leadership, Semco grew from USD$4 million to over USD$160 million in about 20 years. In a 2014 TED Global presentation, Semler said:

'We looked at it and we said, let's devolve to these people, let's give these people a company where we take away all the boarding school aspects of, this is when you arrive, this is how you dress, this is how you go to meetings, this is what you say, this is what you don't say, and let's see what's left ... And so the question we were asking was, how can we be taking care of people? People are the only thing we have.'[5]

Let go

Organizations have to be able to respond quickly to ever-changing conditions. Leaders need to get out of the way and let go of the control. Organizations can only be responsive when they flatten the structure, remove the bureaucracy that slows them down, and give employees autonomy. Decision-making is distributed and communication flows easily throughout the organization. Employee innovation, creativity, and experimentation are embraced. Employees can self-manage. They decide what to work on, how, and when.

One of the biggest challenges facing organizations wishing to create this autonomous workplace is getting managers to let go. Managers need to become leaders and surrender control. Winning soccer teams do not have managers and coaches who are controlling. Winning teams never did anything great because they were told to. Managers and coaches harness the power of teamwork and collaboration, which has a compounding effect when everyone works together to achieve a common goal.

If managers and coaches are too involved with the minutiae of a team's development, they will miss the bigger picture. They have to take a step back and view things objectively.

Permission

Organizations need to evolve constantly if they are going to survive in a world of constant change. They will have to evolve to remain relevant. The old approach of episodic change (discontinuous and intermittent) driven from the top is broken.

Soccer games evolve with twists and turns that no one could predict, and the players continually adapt to the changing conditions. They do not need permission to do so.

The competitive advantage lays in the capacity to change constantly, which comes from employees being equipped with the capability and permission to identify, initiate, and drive change. It is only through constant evolution that the organization will survive and thrive.

Energy and ideas come from the whole of the organization and are the catalyst for change. Transformation requires permission and participation at all levels. The organization will only evolve by working through others. It is power with, not power over.

Give it up

If the organization is going to flatten the structure, evolve, and empower employees, one of the biggest challenges will be overcoming the reluctant leaders who believe that delegation and empowerment of employees means loss of control.

In our turbulent world of constant change, leaders have to move from a *command and control* approach to a *delegate and trust* approach. The *command and control* approach is fine for improving operational efficiency in a well-defined environment.

However, in today's fast moving and complex world, we need to relinquish control in order to gain control. We need to 'give it up'.

Many leaders fear they will lose control if they relinquish control to others. In times of stress, the tendency is to revert to *command and control* while still wanting employees to be creative and innovative and be able to respond rapidly to change.

The issue is that employees will not be creative, innovative, and responsive and are likely to leave the organization if they don't feel trusted and respected.

Leaders must distribute authority and get out of the way.

Carlo Ancelotti is noted as one of the best soccer managers of all time. With over 20 trophies to his name, he is one of the most decorated managers. His style is noted as one of collaboration, versatility, and adaptability. He plays team formations that suit the attributes of his players, and then he gets out of the way.

Adaptive leadership and leadership teams

Not only do leaders need to give up control, they need to become adaptive leaders.

Acknowledging that we are living in a volatile, uncertain, complex, and ambiguous world, how can leaders chart a course when they cannot predict the outcome of their choices?

Today, every organization is an information business. Leaders need to be able to read the right signals and act upon them.

Adaptive leaders learn through experimentation; they manage the context, not the instruction set. They cultivate diversity of view to generate multiplicity of options. They lead with empathy, reward accomplishment with autonomy and seek winning solutions for all stakeholders. Adaptive leaders know what to do when they don't know what to do.

Successful organizations also need adaptive leadership teams. Leadership at the top is now a team effort. Top teams must be more than just high performing. They need to adapt and thrive, regardless of the turbulence they face.

Adaptive leaders and leadership teams enable the success of the organization. Adaptive organizations will outperform their peers when change is volatile and be able to sustain performance going forward.

A great example of adaptable leadership is Chelsea Football Club manager Antonio Conte. After defeat to Arsenal in September 2017, Conte famously switched formation to a 3–4–3, prompting a long unbeaten run that effectively won Chelsea the English Premier League title. Only an adaptive leader would get a veteran group of players, stuck in their ways, to go along with it.[6]

The need for speed

We have a *need for speed*. The only way to be truly responsive to constant change is to become more agile. We had better be ready to manage the people side of rapid change. It is time to release our waterfall ways.

Increasing business demand means agile transformations and iterative implementations; therefore, organizations are now challenged with managing the people side of such fast-paced change. It's not enough to rely on communications and training alone. Many existing change management models follow waterfall rather than agile practices.

The waterfall approach to change won't work on an *agile* project because an agile project won't know the end state until close to the release. Organizational change management needs to align with agile practices in order to manage change during iterative development cycles. Challenges for organizational change are time, information, and planning. None of which are as available as they used to be. Therefore, it is important to build change along the way, and keep pace with the sprint development schedule and evolving cadence.

Organizational change has to match the rhythm so that agile and organizational change become one.

Game score

Soccer teams are perfectly structured to manage players through constant change. The managers, coaches, and players form a winning coalition. The structure is flat with distributed decision-making. Every player can make a decision to achieve the outcome of winning the game without recourse to the coach or manager. They have autonomy to lead.

The manager does not succeed through a *command and control* approach of leadership but surrenders control and allows the players to be innovative and creative.

Managers, coaches, and players have to continually adapt to the changing conditions in which they find themselves and be able to respond in a timely manner—quicker than ever before.

Can you imagine a winning soccer team where only the manager could make decisions, initiate change and develop the ideas? I doubt it. That team would be relegated out of existence.

The same will happen to organizations that don't accept that constant change is the new black and evolve accordingly.

PART 2

PEOPLE TRANSITIONS

CHAPTER 2

Game on

In this chapter, we will explore the roles we need in an organization to successfully transition people through change in a VUCA world.

Keep it simple

There are many change management roles cited in the various change management approaches and frameworks in use today. I have collated a list from the various seminars and workshops I have run with change management leaders and practitioners.

- Executive sponsors
- Primary sponsors
- Reinforcing sponsors
- Sponsors
- Agents
- Champions
- Catalysts
- Targets

- Experience owners
- Change managers
- Change critics
- Change advisors
- Change analysts
- Change specialists
- Change consultants
- Change advocates
- Change leaders
- Stakeholders.

We have recently introduced 'way maker', 'context setter', and 'journey planner' to the list. We need to keep it simple. We do not have time to put together a detailed sponsorship model that identifies every person in the organization who needs to be a sponsor for one particular change and then determine their capability to be an effective sponsor, which then informs a program of work to enable them to be effective sponsors.

Nor do we have time to examine every stakeholder group for every project and categorically determine their position on a change continuum to inform a detailed program of work to move them along the change continuum.

Finally, we do not have time to develop detailed and paper laden plans including:

- Master change management plans
- Communication plans
- Sponsor model and roadmaps
- Coaching plans

- Resistance management plans
- Training plans.

By the time we have done all that, the project has moved on.

A base for constant change

If you are lucky enough to have infinite experienced organizational change management resources; managers with sufficient capacity to sponsor multiple and multi-faceted programs of work; and you are dexterous enough to assess stakeholder positions on many change continuums for each of the changes they are experiencing, maybe, just maybe, this approach is possible.

Meanwhile, for us mere mortals, this is not the case. We have limited resources and capacity.

It's time to wake up and face the world we are living in and determine how we can successfully absorb all of the change that is hitting us while being able to change direction quickly.

We need a base on which anyone can initiate change, where decision-making is delegated, and where people are encouraged to experiment and innovate. Change is not driven from the top and rolled out. Change is embraced. Everyone can set priorities, determine problems and issues, and generate solutions to overcome them. Everyone has the ability to suggest alternatives. Remember, people don't resist change, they resist decrees from on high.

Organizational change becomes a movement rather than a campaign. It is a solid base for constant change; it is not a program. My *Constant Change Transitions Model* below shows how to build a resilient team in the face of constant and relentless change.

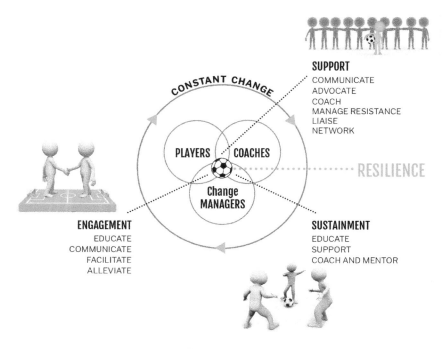

SUPPORT
COMMUNICATE
ADVOCATE
COACH
MANAGE RESISTANCE
LIAISE
NETWORK

CONSTANT CHANGE

PLAYERS   COACHES

Change
MANAGERS

RESILIENCE

ENGAGEMENT
EDUCATE
COMMUNICATE
FACILITATE
ALLEVIATE

SUSTAINMENT
EDUCATE
SUPPORT
COACH AND MENTOR

Constant Change Transitions Model

Organizations need to 'transform' in order to truly have a base upon which everyone has resilience to change. This includes flattening the structure, managers letting go of control, increased employee autonomy and authority, and building a culture of evolution rather than episodic change.

Roles

There are only three roles needed in organizations to manage constant change. They are managers, coaches, and players. (I am using a soccer analogy but you can align these three roles with most field sports.)

As an introduction, a summary of each role within the organization is as follows.

Managers are our organizational change management subject matter experts. They are the people who form our centre of excellence and are the roles we would refer to today as change leads, change practitioners, or change managers.

Managers ensure we are building, maintaining, and sustaining resilience across our workforce (our players).

Managers determine the strategy that is going to be played out; they direct the gameplay. They provide instruction and motivation. Managers ensure that coaches are receiving education and training, support, and coaching and mentoring, so that they can effectively and efficiently transition players through constant change.

Coaches ensure that the players (our workforce) are game fit. They develop the skills and capabilities of the players. Coaches are the active coalition of change agents and sponsors. Coaches are advocates, facilitators, motivators, mediators and advisors.

Managers ensure that coaches truly understand what organizational change management is about. Being a coach is more than having a lanyard that says 'change coach'. Coaches communicate the strategy and game plan that players are being asked to fulfill. They are change sponsors supporting and reinforcing constant change as the norm.

Players are our workforce who will ultimately win or lose the game. It is the players who actually make things happen. They use the gameplay and capabilities with which they have been equipped to win the game.

Change is constant for players. Every match played is different to the one before.

They don't resist constant change; they say 'Game on!'

We have a winning team when we have a coalition of managers, coaches, and players who are all working towards building resilience to change, and when organizational change management is baked into the DNA of the organization and not something added on as an afterthought.

The managers, coaches, and players are a coalition with each traversing the other.

Managers engage with the players and vice versa. Managers sustain the coaches and the coaches provide continual feedback to the managers. The coaches support the players and the players provide continual feedback to the coaches.

Just like a soccer manager, coach, and players will plan the game play together, our change managers and coaches work with players to build change resilience. There is common understanding because change is not being 'done' to anyone, it is being done 'with' them. They work together on the tactics that will be played out in order to win.

After every game there is a game review as to what went well, what didn't, and what will be done differently in the next game. As a collective, the managers, coaches, and players work on continual improvement and ways to maintain and sustain resilience to constant change.

Game score

Unless organizations simplify the roles involved in organizational change management, and structure the team to deal effectively with constant change, failure will result.

Change is constant for the team, and the managers, coaches, and players all work together to create a resilient team.

'Game on!'

CHAPTER 3

Engagement: Managers and players

This section will explore, in depth, the role of the manager in relation to the players in this coalition.

The managers are our subject matter experts in organizational change: the change managers, practitioners, and leaders. They form the organizational change management competency (or center of excellence) within the organization. The competency is furnished with skilled and equipped managers who have capability and credibility, and an enterprise view of change.

They know the terrain and have the experience and expertise to navigate the complexity that is change. Their aim is to continually develop change management competencies throughout the organization and enable the organization to successfully transition through constant change.

The manager's role is about **engagement.** This means they educate, communicate, facilitate, and alleviate.

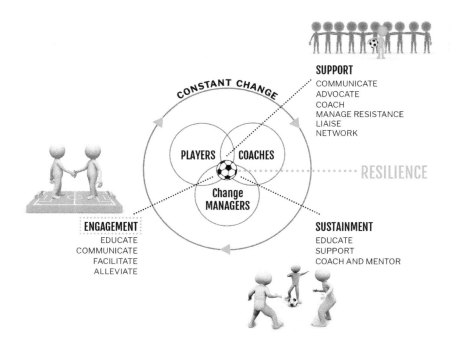

Constant Change Transitions Model: **Engagement**

Educate

The managers provide education for the players.

VUCA

Our players (our workforce) need to understand and embrace the fact that we are living in a volatile, uncertain, complex, and ambiguous world. This is now our reality.

Players need to understand that for the organization to thrive (let alone survive), they need to be resilient to constant change. The need for constant change is being driven by increasing demand from customers, consumers, constituents, and competition.

Not only is this being felt in commercially driven organizations but also in not-for-profit organizations and government agencies. If these organizations are not able to meet the increasing demands of their various stakeholders, those stakeholders will seek alternative solutions and those organizations will cease to remain relevant.

Change leadership

Managers have to educate the entire workforce to become change leaders. When change is constant, leadership of change cannot be placed in the hands of a few. Change has to be everyone's business. Managers and coaches work to help the players embrace constant change as the norm and adapt by building personal competencies such as self-awareness, self-management, resilience, and leadership.

Change leaders are developed at every level. Succeeding in a VUCA world means that leading change has to be everyone's business.

Personal resilience

When change is constant and increasing in speed, players need to know how to build personal resilience to overcome the stress that comes with it. If our workforce cannot build personal resilience, it can result in disengagement, depression, absenteeism, burnout, and other health issues.

Education may include how to exercise mindfulness and make it a core competency within the organization. Mindfulness has been proven to enhance cognitive flexibility and facilitate job performance. Education may also include increasing mental agility and the ability to have empathy both for oneself and others.

Everyone should be educated to identify the signs of stress and know where to seek help.

Solid base for constant change

Organizational change is no longer about a program for change driven from the top and cascaded through the organization. That is too slow in a truly agile world.

Organizations have to establish a solid base for constant change. This is a base upon which everyone can initiate and drive change. Everybody can make decisions. Education is required so that everyone understands employee autonomy and what it means for the organization.

Organizations need to set guardrails or principles for driving change and making decisions. Guardrails keep everyone on the road. The guardrails could be as simple as:

* Do right by the customer.

* Do right by my colleagues.

* Do right by the company.

If you can tick all of those boxes when making a decision or initiating a change, then it's a green light. If the initiative fails, there are no repercussions as the intent was right. Learn from it and move on.

Zappos, the highly successful online shoe retailer has ten core values or principles that employees live by.[1]

1. Deliver WOW through service.

2. Embrace and drive change.

3. Create fun and a little weirdness.

4. Be adventurous, creative, and open-minded.

5. Pursue growth and learning.

6. Build open and honest relationships with communication.

7. Build a positive team and family spirit.

8. Do more with less.

9. Be passionate and determined.

10. Be humble.

When making a decision, Zappos employees know that they can do what it takes to deliver WOW, have the autonomy to make change, and that it is ok to do things differently. When dealing with customers and wondering what to say, they know that principle number 6 is the driving guardrail—be open and honest.

The players (and coaches) need education around autonomy and the guardrails.

Communication

Managers need to ensure there is two-way communication and appropriate channels for communication and collaboration. Enterprise social networks (ESN) play a key role in effective communication and collaboration. Examples include Yammer, Jive, and Slack.

Guardrails and principles

Managers should ensure that communication includes reinforcement of the guardrails and principles that guide decision-making and initiation of change.

Constant change

Communication should include regular reminders of the need to maintain personal resilience and that living in a VUCA world is now our reality.

Continual feedback loops

Communication enables continual feedback loops where players and coaches provide feedback to managers (and vice versa) about what is working well, what is not working well, and what can be improved. Just as the field team is debriefed after every match (where feedback is exchanged), the same needs to happen on a regular and ad-hoc basis in the workplace.

Facilitate

Managers need to provide supporting resources for players to cope with constant and rapid change. These resources include knowledge, support, tools, and training.

Whatever resources are provided, it is imperative that they are easily accessible. Resources need to be easy to find and navigate.

Managers are responsible for the maintenance and continual improvement of resources to ensure a change-ready and resilient organization.

Alleviate

Managers should seek to alleviate the pressure of constant change by increasing the organizational change management capability at every level in the organization.

Coaching and mentoring should be available to everyone in the organization.

Managers will ensure that leading edge solutions are in place to assist the workforce deal with constant and rapid change. When needed, managers will be accountable for obtaining additional resources to support the organization and future-proof it for constant change.

Game score

The change practitioners (the managers) have to stop doing and start strategizing. Organizational change can no longer be the responsibility of a few. The whole team (managers, coaches, and players) has to be accountable.

Managers have capability and credibility, and an enterprise view of change. They are educators, communicators, and facilitators, and they work to alleviate the pressure of constant change.

CHAPTER 4

Sustainment: Managers and coaches

Here, we explore the role of the manager in relation to the coaches. The coaches are our change network, change champions, change agents or change advocates. They can be called many things but in the world of constant change, they truly need to be change coaches.

Managers ensure that coaches really understand what organizational change management is about. The manager's role is about sustainment. The managers sustain the ability of the coaches to be effective in their role of transitioning the players through the complexity that is constant change.

Coaches can exist in all levels within the organization. Coaches form an active network and a movement that embeds organizational change management into the fabric of the organization so that it becomes intrinsic.

Coaches are open to feedback and new ideas, and they are often, though not always, quite creative. They embrace change, think critically, and are not afraid to move away from how things have always been done.

Coaches communicate the strategy and game plan that players are being asked to fulfill.

Sustainment means that managers educate, support, coach, and mentor.

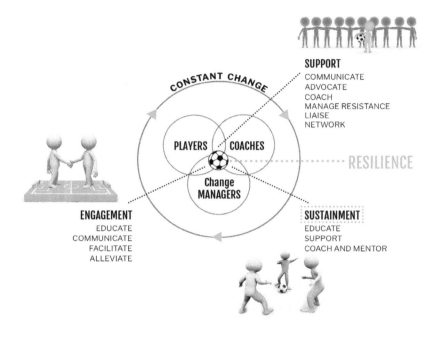

Constant Change Transitions Model: **Sustainment**

Educate

Managers will ensure the currency of coaches' proficiency and plan for future needs. Coaches will inform managers of any additional education, training, resources, and capabilities they require to undertake their role effectively.

VUCA

Managers need to ensure that coaches have the skills, knowledge, and capability to facilitate the acceptance of constant change as the norm throughout the organization. Just as the managers educate the players that we are now operating in a VUCA world, the coaches need the same education. Coaches also need to embrace the new reality.

Change coaches

Coaches need education about what it means to be a 'true' coach and build a resilient workforce. They need to know how the organization works and understand its challenges and strengths. They also need to be 'tuned in' to the mood of different areas of the organization and be able to provide clarification about constant change.

They need to be able to focus on behavioral change to make the workforce resilient to constant change and help people embrace and adapt to constant change by building personal competencies. As well as listening skills, they need 'looking' skills. A person's body language can tell us a lot about their emotional state. Sometimes the answer is right in front of us.

Coaches need to be able to provide feedback to the players and the managers.

Coaches need to be able to act on their intuition. Sometimes they can get a sudden thought or feeling about a player or players. It feels like a hunch or second sense. Coaches need to have the confidence to trust that feeling and act upon it in the hope that it will help the players.

Communication

Coaches need education and support to become effective communicators and listeners. They need questioning techniques to understand the reality of players' perceptions. They need to empathize.

Coaches need to entrench the message that constant change is the new norm. They need to prepare the players with behaviors, attitudes, skills, and communication to deal with constant change.

Coaches need to continually check back in with both the players and the managers that everything is on track to achieve the end goal.

Support

Managers need to provide unremitting support for coaches. Coaches (and players) operate in times of instability and uncertainty. They need the ability to remain highly effective under intense pressure.

Coaches need the education, skills, and capability, with which they have been equipped, to be underpinned by unrelenting support from managers.

Support goes further than formal training. Managers can create collaboration platforms using tools such as Slack, Jive or Yammer, where coaches can support each other and managers can provide additional knowledge.

Managers need to check-in consistently on the health and well-being of the coaches and provide required support and intervention in a timely manner.

Just as the coaches need good communication, listening, and empathy skills, the managers need the same in order to provide effective support to the coaches.

Support also involves managers understanding what motivates the coaches and incorporating that into their management approach. Managers should acknowledge and reward coaches for the good work they do.

Overall, managers have to show that they care about the coaches, work alongside them (not over them), be real and transparent, and make time for them. Managers need to be available always to the coaches.

Coach and mentor

Managers are coaches and mentors to the coaches.

Coach

Coaching will focus on addressing known issues and developing skills. This could include communication skills and building networks. The manager teaches the coach how to develop these skills. The aim of coaching is to improve individual performance.

Mentor

Mentoring provides a safe environment where the coach can share issues affecting their professional and personal success.

Although specific learning goals or competencies may be used as a basis for creating the relationship, its focus goes beyond those areas to include work/life balance, self-confidence, self-perception, and how the personal influences the professional.

Mentoring helps develop the coach in their current and future roles. Mentoring, alongside education and coaching, may identify the managers of the future.

Game score

Our coaches form our change network. They are true change coaches and exist in all levels of the organization.

Coaches really understand what organizational change management is about.

They form an active network and a movement that embeds organizational change management into the fabric of the organization so that it becomes intrinsic.

CHAPTER 5

Support: Coaches and players

Now we explore the role of the coaches in relation to the players.

Our coaches are our constant change advocates; they are a movement.

Coaches are at every level across the organization. Coaches work with the managers to build change resilience into our players (our workforce). We need our workforce to be like a winning soccer team.

Think about an individual player on a team. Every game they play is different. So what changes?

- Ground
- Pitch
- Playing conditions
- Weather
- Supporters
- Opposition

- Game tactics
- Team composition
- Playing positions.

During the game itself, things might change:

- Playing positions
- Opposition tactics
- Game tactics
- Team numbers (if red carded).

The players do not resist these changes. They say 'Game on!' Constant change is the norm for the players. At the end of the day, the players will win or lose the game.

The managers and the coaches work to build change resilience into the workforce.

The coach's role is about unrelenting support for the players. The coaches build change resilience through support.

Support means that coaches communicate, advocate, coach, manage resistance, liaise, and network.

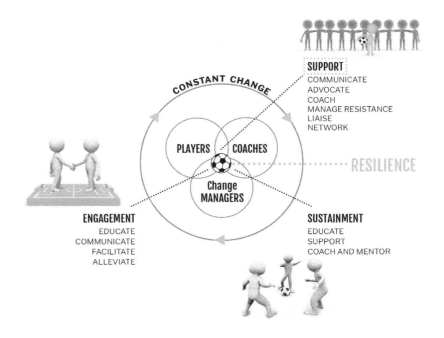

SUPPORT
COMMUNICATE
ADVOCATE
COACH
MANAGE RESISTANCE
LIAISE
NETWORK

CONSTANT CHANGE

PLAYERS COACHES

Change
MANAGERS

RESILIENCE

ENGAGEMENT
EDUCATE
COMMUNICATE
FACILITATE
ALLEVIATE

SUSTAINMENT
EDUCATE
SUPPORT
COACH AND MENTOR

Constant Change Transitions Model: **Support**

Communicate

There has to be organization-wide acceptance that constant change is the new norm. Coaches communicate clear and unambiguous messages. Coaches use their expertise to share knowledge and steer players in the right direction.

Their communication skills include active listening, empathy, and analysis. They actively look for clues to why players are not moving in the intended direction. Coaches listen and encourage players. Their communication motivates and inspires the players.

A key role of the coaches is to articulate consistently and regularly the compelling reasons why change has to be constant. They will carefully craft and customize their messages to increase their chances to inspire and motivate people into sustained efforts and resilience.

They stimulate meaningful conversations and ensure that communication is a two way process. They will utilize enterprise social networks such as Yammer, Jive or Slack to enable active and real-time collaboration and communication.

Autonomy

Communication, alongside advocacy and coaching, will aim to instill autonomy into everyone in the organization, including the players. Autonomy means that decision-making is decentralized and placed where it is best needed.

In a world of constant and rapid change, there isn't time for decision-making and change initiatives to go up and down the chain of command. By the time they do, the world has moved on. Everyone has to be able to make decisions and drive change if the organization is going to survive. Therefore, the players have autonomy. (However, this does not result in anarchy. The guardrails or principles that mitigate this have already been explained.)

A player does not wait until half time and then inform the coach that they had a great idea that would most likely have resulted in a goal but didn't want to make that decision until they had conferred. The opportunity has now passed and the good idea is irrelevant.

The players make decisions in real time with the right intentions and if things don't work out as planned there are no adverse repercussions. It is all about learning from those experiences and moving on.

Meaningful conversations

Coaches will have meaningful conversations with players. Coaches should always aim to get the most out of conversations but even more so in a fast-paced, ever-changing environment. Bringing meaning to conversations will build better relationships.

Meaningful conversations include asking meaningful questions and getting over the chitchat. Coaches show they are genuinely interested and want to hear what the other person has to say. Coaches will find out what interests the other person and dig deeper. They will ask for stories not answers.

Coaches will have meaningful conversations that uncover the other person's goals, ambitions, drivers etc. and further build the relationship. Coaches will be vulnerable and transparent, share experiences, find common ground, and demonstrate empathy. Coaches will validate the other person's experiences.

Coaches will ask players for their thoughts and advice on various topics, which brings mindfulness into the conversation.

Advocate

Coaches are advocates for constant change. Coaches are our sponsors. The traditional approach to sponsorship, when change was episodic, was for the change management experts to determine the person best suited to be the primary sponsor for a particular initiative. This would usually be a senior leader or executive.

The change management experts would then determine the positions between the impacted stakeholder groups and the primary sponsor also required to sponsor the change.

Once all the required sponsors had been identified, the change management experts would then determine (a) the position of the sponsor in relation to the change (i.e. for, against, neutral) and (b) the capability of the identified sponsor to be an effective sponsor.

Depending on the results of (a) and (b), the change experts would take action to either make the sponsors advocates of the change and/or build the required sponsorship capabilities.

Clearly, both identification of the sponsors and resulting actions required, could take a significant amount of time.

In our world of constant and rapid change, we no longer have the luxury of building a sponsorship coalition/model in this manner for every initiative.

Coaches are the sponsors for constant change. Coaches are active sponsors for every initiative that is taking place across the organization. They evangelize the fact that constant change is the new norm; they are vocal and persistent. They are public and untiring champions for constant change. They actively urge, promote, espouse, and support acceptance of the new norm.

Coach

Coaches provide the players with ongoing and continual coaching.

Coaching allows the players the personal space and support they need to grow and develop. The coach's key role is often to maintain the motivation and commitment needed to win the game.

The coaches will require sound knowledge and understanding of the organization, its objectives, values, and desired outcomes. They possess a variety of styles, skills, and techniques appropriate to the context in which the coaching is taking place.

At all times, coaches remain non-judgmental and supportive of the players. Coaches ensure that the players develop the individual competencies they need to have resilience in a world of constant change.

Manage resistance

It is time to stop talking about resistance to change and start talking about resilience to change. The only resistance the coach should be managing is resistance to the fact that change is constant. They need to assist the players in embracing the new world of instability and unknowns.

Resistance to change has customarily been associated with change being done *to* the various stakeholders rather than being done *with* the stakeholders. Lack of communication and collaboration in regards to the reason for change has also contributed to resistance.

In today's world, the adoption of an agile mindset in which customer collaboration is king, means that nothing is done unless it is the 'right' thing to do by the customer.

Add to that, the agile values:[1]

'Our highest priority is to satisfy the customer through early and continuous delivery of valuable software.'

'Welcome changing requirements, even late in development, agile processes harness change for the customer's competitive advantage.'

'Business people and developers must work together daily throughout the project.'

If these values are intrinsic, resistance to change should be minimized as change is being done *with* individuals through interactions and the customer is driving the change.

When it is determined that requirements need to change (at any point) due to competition, customer and consumer demands, technology advancements etc., the changes are made.

The old list of reasons people resist change are mitigated in our new world.

OLD WORLD	NEW WORLD
Lack of awareness/understanding of the reason for change	Continual collaboration and communication
Fear of the unknown	Acceptance that unknown unknowns are the reality
	Resilience
Impact on current job/role	Continual collaboration and communication
	Self-organizing teams
	Autonomy
	Environment and support needed for players
	Coaching
Change fatigue	Resilience
	Coaching
Lack of competence	Coaches ensure competency and skills
Lack of visible support and commitment	Coaches as active, visible, and unrelenting sponsors
Organization's past performance with change	Acknowledgement of past performance and constant and collaborative reflection on how to improve

Change Resistance Mitigation

Liaise

Coaches are the hub of liaison between the managers and the players. This does not prevent direct liaison between players and managers. As on the playing field, coaches liaise with the managers to determine game play and convey that information to the players. They also receive feedback from the players that is conveyed to the managers.

Information conveyed to managers could include change fitness, player health, changes in opposition (competition), playing conditions, tactical improvements, skill requirements, validation of game plan etc.

There are continuous feedback loops between managers, coaches, and players.

The feedback loops mean that the results of playing the game are allowed to influence how the game is played in the future.

Network

Coaches are central to the organizational network to enable change resilience.

Due to the complexity and volatile nature of change that is likely to be divergent, coaches will build bridging networks that connect players to other players who aren't yet connected. Bridging networks connect the unconnected and the outliers.

The benefits are that coaches get access to new information and knowledge instead of hearing the same thing repeatedly.

In building networks, coaches can seek out players that will make excellent coaches and thus increase the coaching network by facilitating that transition. Coaches can mobilize others by sharing information, knowledge, opportunities, and support.

Coaches seek to grow the coaching network organically.

Game score

The coaches provide unrelenting support for the players. They build change resilience through support.

Support means that coaches communicate, advocate, coach, manage resistance, liaise, and network.

Our coaches will operate like soccer coaches during training sessions. They will:

- Observe from the sideline.
- Pause the game (when possible) if an error is spotted or the game is not flowing as expected.
- *Ask* the players what the problem is (instead of telling them).
- Explore options.
- Ensure players can demonstrate understanding.
- Get in and out quickly.
- Try it out.
- Get off the field, and let play continue.
- If it's not working, celebrate the learning, and try something else.

Players do not resist change. They say 'Game on!'

PART 3

KILL THE HIERARCHY

CHAPTER 6

The winning team

Without the luxury of taking a breath after each change and preparing for the next, we have to build an organization comprised of managers, coaches, and players who embrace the new world and for whom constant change is just the way things are.

This is the winning team. They say, 'Game On!'

In the following chapters, I will describe the actions that organizations need to undertake to create a resilient workforce. I will explain why the hierarchy must be removed or reduced and how leaders must let go of control and get out of the way. I will also discuss the permission we need to give our players to play the game as they see fit, and how we need to build adaptive leaders and teams that can sense and respond to constant change.

Our organizational change managers may not be able to address all of these alone. However, with an effective change network of coaches, the change managers can start to explore strategies needed to build the required resilience.

Change managers will work with organizational development, human resources, executives and the C-suite to affect the change necessary if the organization is going to meet the increasing demands being placed upon them.

Change or die

The key message from the change managers is that if the organization does not change, it is looking at irrelevance and obsolescence. If the organization is going to survive, it has to build a resilient workforce through deconstruction and then reconstruction.

But the organization must do this before constant, relentless, and rapid change becomes its new reality. That means now.

For an organization to survive and thrive in a world of constant and uncertain change, the organization has to be one in which leadership is important, but MORE important is a collaborative workplace in which transparency and creative freedom reign over hierarchical boundaries. This enables innovation, creativity, experimentation, rapid decision-making, agility, and employee ownership, engagement, and influence. There must be widespread autonomy where everyone leads.

A winning soccer team is one in which everyone leads and players have autonomy to win the game though collaboration, innovation, and creativity. Decisions are made rapidly, and the players own the outcome. Great players think for themselves.

No one ever did anything awesome or great just because they were told to.

MOVING TO A FLATTER STRUCTURE

The only way to enable a 'faster' organization that can respond to constant change is to flatten the structure. It needs to move away from a structure of hierarchical control to a flatter structure that removes the bureaucracy that slows organizations down. It's not about having no structure or hierarchy at all.

The *Kill the Hierarchy Model* below illustrates the changes needed to move to a flatter structure.

Valve Corporation (a leading video game developer and digital distribution system) and Morning Star (a leading food processor) have moved to a 'completely flat' structure. Whereas, some organizations like W.L. Gore, Facebook, Pixar, and Toyota have moved to a 'flatter' structure.

Whether organizations move to a completely flat structure or a flatter structure, informal hierarchies will emerge just as they do in nature. However, this type of hierarchy is very different from the social constructs we impose with the sole intention of 'keeping control'.

However, 'flat organizations' aren't truly 'flat'. They are just flatter than tall organizations. Tall organizations shift the responsibility up the management ladder; whereas, flatter structures empower employees to make decisions and feel responsible for the organization's success.

Characteristics of flatter structure organizations include an increased level of communication between employees and management, greater democracy, and a greater level of innovation. Communication is usually faster, more reliable, and more effective than in tall structures. Direct employee input leads to more support for decisions and fewer behind-the-scenes power struggles and disagreements.

Who's doing it?

The Gore website states:[1]

'We also have a leadership structure. Leaders most often emerge based on skill, capability and followership — or their potential to build followership over time. The leadership structure helps us understand expectations and scope and helps each of us stay accountable to our commitments.'

At Morning Star, rather than pushing decisions up, expertise is pushed down. In many organizations, senior executives trained in the science of business analytics make the key decisions. They have a wealth of data at their disposal and analytical prowess, but what they lack is context—an understanding of the reality and facts at the coalface. This is why decisions that appear brilliant by the top-level executives are seen as idiotic by those on the front line. Roughly half of the employees at Morning Star have completed courses on how to negotiate with suppliers and financial analysis. This puts the doers and the thinkers at the same level so that decisions are faster and wiser.

Valve, considered one of the most successful companies within its industry, has approximately 250 employees and an estimated worth of USD$5 billion. Rather than assigning permanent managerial staff, Valve rotates its leaders on a per-team, per-project basis. Rather than creating permanent departments, Valve allows employees to choose the type of work they want to do.

Why are they doing it?

A flatter structure suits organizations that are looking to innovate, needing to respond to rapid and constant change and wanting a shared sense of purpose.

When employees have influence and can actively participate in decision-making, they have a sense of ownership. The flatter structure empowers employees, and as they take on a bigger role within the organization, they become increasingly motivated to be successful. Reducing middle management means there are fewer layers between the most senior level and the front-line employees. This makes it easier to communicate and drive change.

When we allow self-management, individuals take responsibility for their own actions and behaviors. At Morning Star, the managerial functions of planning, organizing, staffing, directing, and controlling are the personal responsibility of each employee.

The Morning Star Self-Management Institute article *What Is Self Management?* describes the key ideas central to the self-management philosophy:[2]

- *People are generally happier when they have control over their own life (and work).*

- *It doesn't make a lot of sense to give the decision-making authority to the person farthest (literally) away from the actual work being done.*

- *When you give good people more responsibility, they tend to flourish.*

- *The traditional hierarchical model of organizations is not scalable—in fact, it's a recipe for a slow painful death.*

- *There's an undeniable link between freedom and economic prosperity in nations around the world—and, further, an undeniable link between lack of freedom and corruption at the national level. The same is true of human organizations in general.*

Game score

To successfully transition people and the organization through constant change, we need to remove the bureaucracy, flatten the hierarchy, speed up decision-making, empower and involve employees, and give control to those who are actually doing the work.

No soccer team is going to win without rapid decision-making and player autonomy to do the right thing in order to outplay the competition.

If organizations are earnest about building a resilient workforce, they will have to deconstruct in order to reconstruct. There is no Band-Aid solution. For many organizations, this will be open-heart surgery.

CHAPTER 7

Rapid decision-making

In a hierarchy, decisions can take a long time due to the layers through which information has to flow before a decision is made. When organizations need to respond quickly to changing priorities, opportunities, competition, threats etc. the ability to make decisions quickly will be essential for success. Therefore, the hierarchy has to be flattened so there are less decision-making hoops through which to jump.

As a soccer player, the speed of decision-making is paramount to team success. Ultimately, imagination and the speed of thought/decision-making is the most important quality any player can possess. We need to give our players the freedom to make decisions.

When fewer people have to be consulted about a decision, it allows for provision of rapid response to issues or concerns. A flatter structure creates a direct communication line between the head of the organization (e.g. CEO) and the employees on the front line. Quality decisions can be made rapidly as they have context based on reality informed by the 'workers'.

Decision driven structure

An organizations performance is reliant on its ability to make decisions better and faster than the competition.

The organizational structure should reflect the organizations strategic priorities. If the organization needs to be more innovative, the structure needs to enable decision-making that drives increased innovation over time.

It's essential to identify the decisions that will be significant in the success of the organization and then determine where in the organization those decisions should be made in order to create the most value.

Digital disadvantage

The increased ease and reduced cost of communication in the digital age has made decision-making worse. It is easy to bring more and more people into the decision-making process through email and collaboration platforms while not being clear about where the decision-making authority actual resides. The outcome is too many meetings and too many email threads that do not add any value. Add to that the fact that we now have more information than we know what to do with, coming from more and more diverse sources.

What is needed is a flatter organization to make decision-making faster. Decision-making is distributed and placed in the hands of those best placed to make the decision. Decision-making is placed where the reaction or anticipation of a change in the business environment can be responded to immediately.

Decision-making best placed

The more hierarchical (and bureaucratic) an organization becomes, the more it opens itself up to slow *and* bad decision-making.

The taller the hierarchy gets, the ability of those with the knowledge to contest rightly to a questionable decision, reduces. When the magnitude of power increases in relation to a position in the hierarchy and is not based on knowledge, expertise, experience, or capability, decision-making can be a risky business. The person making such a decision is likely to be the person situated farthest from the reality, relevance, and context in which the decision should be made. Decisions made from the peak of the mountain are often impractical at base camp.

The hierarchical organization disempowers those best suited to make informed and rapid decisions. Not only does the decision-making reduce to a snail's pace, it also decreases in quality.

Decision-making needs to be placed where the people most capable to make quick and educated decisions are situated.

The Morning Star website states:[1]

> 'We envision an organization of self-managing professionals who initiate communication and coordination of their activities with fellow colleagues, customers, suppliers, and fellow industry participants, absent directives from others.'

Morning Star has put the decision-making where it needs to be. Workers are given the tools and empowerment to make decisions in order to carry out their jobs. If you need an $8000 welding machine to do your job, you order it. Business units negotiate customer-supplier agreements and employees can initiate the hiring process when they need additional resources. Decision-making is rapid and not constrained by a hierarchy.

Game score

Rapid decision-making is needed if organizations are going to promptly respond to the volatile and increasingly competitive environment in which it exists. Decision-making needs to be placed in the position best suited to enable a quick reaction and a quality response.

Rapid-decision-making will only be enabled through a flatter and more fluid organizational structure that reduces the unnecessary hierarchy.

Soccer players have to make split second decisions. The disruption in the game means that players have less time to make decisions and decide what to do with the ball. The only position in which the decision can be placed is with the players.

CHAPTER 8

Decentralized decision-making

The flat organizational model promotes employee involvement through decentralized decision-making. It elevates the level of responsibility of front-line employees and eliminates unnecessary layers of management, resulting in comments and feedback reaching all personnel involved in decision-making more quickly.

When the game is in play and the competition is getting dangerously near scoring, the decision-making is with the players, not the managers and coaches. The players have to think on their feet. They anticipate, recognize, and react. Our workforce has to be the same.

The cat is out of the bag

A good example of the benefits of decentralized decision-making comes from the industrial equipment manufacturer Caterpillar. In the 1980s, Caterpillar, fondly known as Cat, began to suffer from its highly centralized decision-making structure. It had a hierarchical bureaucracy that was inward facing and out of touch with the marketplace.

At this time, all the pricing decisions were made in the corporate headquarters in Peoria, Illinois. If a sales representative in South Africa wanted to give a customer a discount on a product, they had to check with headquarters first. To add even more misery, headquarters did not always have accurate or timely information about the subsidiary markets to make an effective decision. As a result, Cat was at the mercy of the competition.

Cat's formerly comfortable position in the marketplace turned into opportunities for competitors like the Japanese firm Komatsu. In 1982, Cat posted its first annual loss of its 50-year history. In order to overcome this centralized paralysis, Cat underwent a number of dramatic rounds of reorganization through the 1990s and 2000s. It reorganized into a flatter structure and recaptured its market shares. The organization moved accountability downward in the organization and dramatically decentralized decision rights.

After posting a $2.4 billion loss in 1992, Cat returned to profitability in 1993 and has increased its earnings ever since. It made record profits of $2 billion in 2004.

Best placed

Increased competitiveness means organizations have to deliver value in the shortest possible time. This requires decentralized decision-making. Decisions that go up the chain of command introduce a delay and decrease in quality as they have a lack of local context. Add to this the fact that during the delay, changes can happen that render the decision superfluous.

When employees make decisions that matter to them, it increases engagement and productivity while also increasing the agility of the organization to respond to change.

Devolved and distributed power

Semco doesn't have a mission statement, written polices, job titles, or an organizational chart. Decision-making is in the hands of the employees. CEO Semler summarized his position on distributed of power when he said:

'We'll send our sons anywhere in the world to die for democracy, but don't seem to apply the concept to the workplace.'[1]

In 1982, at the age of 24, Semler became the CEO of Semco. He slowly began changing the organization from an autocracy to a corporate democracy. He cut the bureaucracy from twelve layers of management to four and devised a new structure based on concentric circles to replace the traditional, confining, corporate pyramid.

The center circle comprises the top five managers called Counselors. The second circle consists of Partners who are in charge of the small business units. Coordinators, whose job it is to supervise, represent the third circle, and the rest are called Associates.

Semler devolved and distributed power. Company revenue, profit margins and salaries are totally transparent with all employees having access. Employees set their own salaries. It is about accountability and performance over hours worked. Employees set their own working hours. They choose their managers and evaluate them twice a year. There are no receptionists, secretaries, or personal assistants.

Semco's core values are:

- Democracy: gives employees control of their work.
- Profit sharing: gives employees a reason to do work better.
- Information: tells employees what is working and what is not.

This didn't happen overnight, and it was a concerted effort over five years to get distribution of power established. Semler also made himself redundant when it came to decision-making. The organization held a party to celebrate the 10th anniversary of the last time he made a decision.

Game score

Decentralized decision-making encourages motivation and creativity; it allows many minds to work simultaneously on the same problem, and it accommodates flexibility and individualization.

Allowing more people to be involved in the decision-making process, increases input for solutions, and innovative ideas.

Power is placed directly into lower areas of the organization. Upper management doesn't get involved, and decisions can be made much faster. Unnecessary escalation to management is just a needless delay. Quality of decisions also diminishes if the decision does not have local context.

When power is placed with the players who are best placed to make the decisions, actions are taken at the speed required in order to win the game. If decisions have to be escalated to the managers, there would be no movement on the field, and the competition would walk away with the victory—literally.

CHAPTER 9

Increased innovation

Innovation has to be a strategic capability.

When two soccer teams, of equal capability, meet, the one that innovates will win the game. Barcelona's Ronaldo (FIFA World Player of the Year in 2004 and 2005 and runner up in subsequent years) said:

> *'The important thing is to keep on innovating and finding a way to surprise. You always look to surprise with dribbling, a new move, a new pass. (...) As long as I believe I have the creativity for that, that's what I'll try and do. I'm never going to lose my characteristics because that's what I know how to do. I want to mix everything that is innovative with the same things as always. Perhaps the fans expect me to do all the tricks, the opponents as well. If you don't innovate, they all take the ball away from you. I believe it's important to innovate in order to avoid repetition.'[1]*

Organizations have to actively encourage and support employees to create, collaborate, innovate, and experiment. They need to feel safe to do so. Everyone needs the confidence and self-assurance to step outside of their comfort zone and try something different in order to respond effectively to business challenges with which they are faced.

Organizations with a flatter structure tend to be much more innovative. If innovation is strategically important to the organization, it needs to be flat(ter).

Innovation for the long haul

At Morning Star, innovation is key to the organization's success.

As the Morning Star website declares:

'At all Morning Star facilities, we emphasize innovative thought, and we strive to use available resources and technology to their fullest potential in order to continuously improve quality, productivity and service for our customer. As important as quality, service and price are, we know there is more. To remain competitive for the long term, we must be innovative. That is why we rigorously maintain our position as the major force developing and implementing new and improved technology in our industry.'[2]

Creative freedom

Innovation is driven by a more collaborative workplace in which transparency and creative freedom are far more important than hierarchical structure and inflexibility.

Organizational hierarchy and top-down structure can prevent employees from actively participating in the innovation process and being creative. Employees can feel intimidated, and fear being judged or chastised for unsuccessful ideas.

Flattening the organization and removing hierarchical barriers recognizes that innovation is driven with input from everyone.

In regards to his dream for W.L. Gore, founder Bill Gore said back in 1961:

> *'I dreamed of an enterprise with great opportunity for all who would join in it, a virile organization that would foster self-fulfillment and which would multiply the capabilities of the individuals comprising it beyond their mere sum.'* [3]

The Gore website says:

> *'The culture of Gore is apparent when you see us work: we collaborate, we innovate, and we're committed — because our success is Gore's, and Gore's success is ours.'*

Gore employs more than 10,000 people in some fifty locations and is consistently ranked one of the best places to work; it is among the most innovative and profitable companies in the world. Gore has no hierarchy, no bosses, and no job titles. At Gore, every employee is known as an 'Associate' and everyone is an owner and accountable for outcomes.

Game score

Hierarchy and centralized decision-making stifles innovation and creativity, both of which are strategic advantages to all organizations. Flat structures are far more likely to innovate.

Companies like Google, Valve, and Toyota have opted for flat structures to create environments that foster innovation.

For organizations to survive and thrive they need to innovate and nurture creativity.

If the players on a soccer team are not allowed to be innovative and creative and, therefore, have the winning advantage, the game will be lost. Winning teams are organized but fluid. They do not play to a rigid system (like a hierarchy) that stifles innovation and creativity.

The Netherlands soccer team brought innovation to the forefront in 1974 when they qualified for the FIFA World Cup Final. They leveraged the tactic of Total Football (discussed later in the book), which meant that any player could take over the role of any other player on the team. When Dutch players switched to different positions, they totally confused the opposition.

Since 1974, when innovation was the key to the success of the Dutch side, it has only reached the World Cup final twice, and in 2018, failed to qualify. They lost their innovative spirit.

This was summed up by past national team manager, Martin Jol, when he said:

'In the Netherlands, our philosophy was to be different. Now we want to be like everybody else — and they are bigger and better than us'[4]

Holland, a country once at the forefront of innovative thinking in soccer, hit the wall with devastating results.

CHAPTER 10

Employee engagement

Employee engagement means that employees have choices and work towards the success of the organization. They are actively involved and enthusiastic about their work and the workplace.

A hierarchical structure can disempower employees. A flatter structure provides more opportunities for employees to be involved in decision-making processes and, therefore, they are increasingly motivated and engaged. Employees have more autonomy.

Managers and coaches work hard to ensure that players are engaged. When players are engaged and motivated, they will win more games and improve their skills faster. Good managers and coaches not only engage and motivate the players on the field but also those on the bench. They ensure the players on the bench know that even if they are not on the field they have an important role to play on the team. They know they could be called, at any point, to join the competition and, therefore, need to be physically and mentally fit. They have a key role in observing the game, anticipating what the opposition could do, and informing the coaches. The managers and coaches ensure there is engagement with the players and that they all know how to 'stay in the game'.

Employee engagement has many benefits.

Benefits

When employees are engaged, job satisfaction increases. Engaged and satisfied employees are invested in the success of the organization and demonstrate a high level of commitment and loyalty. Engaged employees will go the extra mile to achieve business success.

When employees are engaged, there is less absenteeism. They are increasingly motivated hence productivity increases. Having an engaged workforce not only retains talent but also attracts talent to the organization.

The engaged employee is motivated. This leads to increased innovation and creativity. Engaged employees actively collaborate with each other. They look out for each other and the organization. They have a sense of ownership of the outcomes of their work and the success of the organization.

Engagement = loyalty

Employee engagement drives loyalty, and there are inherent cost savings associated with reducing employee attrition. Retaining talent is core to organizational success.

Morning Star focuses on building employee engagement. It is about generating joy and excitement for everyone. Their website states:

'For colleagues to find joy and excitement utilizing their unique talents and to weave those talents into activities which complement and strengthen fellow colleagues' activities. For

colleagues to take personal responsibility and hold themselves accountable for achieving our Mission and shaping the Tomato Game.'[1]

And then there is the bottom line

Morning Star has very low attrition due to high employee engagement. What does employee attrition cost Australian organizations?

According to Workplace Info, if an organization of 500 employees could reduce attrition from 10% to 5% it could save the business over $2.5 million a year.[2]

Their website states:

'A business with 500 employees can expect to have 50 resignations per year. Latest Average Weekly Earnings (AWE) figures issued by the Australian Bureau of Statistics (for November 2015) record AWE for full-time employees of $1,499.30. Adding 30% to this for the cost of employee benefits and on-costs amounts to $449.79, giving a total cost of $1,949.09.

Assuming turnover cost to be a year's total remuneration for each employee, total annual cost of turnover for this business is $1,949.09 x 52 weeks x 50 employees. That's a total of $5,067,634 per year. So a retention strategy that was able to reduce employee resignations from 10% to 5% per year would save this business over $2.5 million per year, less the costs of implementing the strategy.'

Disengagement epidemic

Adecco describes Australia's employee disengagement as an epidemic.[3]

The *Adecco Employment and Talent Report 2016* states that there is one area of business that needs urgent attention: employee engagement. Adecco says:

Disengaged workers remain costly for employers. A significant 76% of Australian workers are in two minds about their jobs, or worse still, are completely disengaged. With only 24% of the workforce engaged, the drain on the wider economy is apparent: disengagement costs the national economy a whopping $54.8 billion annually. This cost can be seen in numerous areas. Disengaged workers have been proven to be:

- **Less profitable**. *Highly engaged employees achieve twice the annual net income of organizations whose employees lag behind on engagement.*

- **Less loyal.** *81% of engaged workers are willing to provide positive recommendations of their employer's services, compared to 18% of the actively disengaged.*

- **Less safe.** *Engaged employees are five times less likely to have a safety incident than disengaged employees and seven times less likely to have an incident requiring time off work.*

- **Less innovative.** *60% of engaged employees say their job sparks creative ideas compared to just 3% of the disengaged.*

Game score

Organizations cannot afford to have disengaged employees. A hierarchical structure can make it difficult for employees lower down in the structure to feel engaged. Therefore, we need to flatten the structure to drive increased engagement. We need to give employees (those who create wealth for the organization) the ability to lead and make independent decisions, which will spur action, innovation, and creativity.

In essence, we are enabling employees to reach the summit of Maslow's Hierarchy of Needs theory from 1943—self-actualization. That's not a new idea now, is it?

The soccer manager, despite being separated from the team while watching from the sideline, is not disengaged. He or she is totally engaged with what is happening on the pitch and how the players are performing. If they are disengaged there will be no motivation, encouragement, support, or energy coming from the sidelines.

If the manager, and coach want to retain the talented players, they have to continually drive engagement so that players don't become disillusioned. A club scout from the opposition will be more than ready to acquire your talent.

CHAPTER 11

Active employees

Active employee involvement increases productivity and profitability. A flat organizational structure empowers employees. When employees take on a greater role within the organization, they become more personally motivated to succeed and are more active in the organization.

When employee voices are heard and their ideas considered, they are more likely to actively share ideas and opinions without the fear of being shut down. When there is a lively exchange of ideas and thoughts, creativity and productivity will increase.

When we are living in a world in which change is rapid and dynamic, the bureaucracy of an entrenched hierarchy will just slow an organization down and leave it vulnerable. Competitors with a flat structure, where employees actively apply their skills where needed and are able to shift effort quickly to match market demand, have a distinct advantage. Employees themselves can shift efforts to where they are most needed for the organization to succeed.

As previously mentioned, soccer teams are made up of players on and off the field. All players, including those on the bench, will be actively involved in applying their skills wherever they can make a difference. This could involve observation of gameplay and making recommendations to the coach. It could involve scouting for new talent, checking out the competition for the next game, checking out individual players considered a potential threat to winning the next game, contributing to gameplay planning and actively and visibly supporting the players on the field. There isn't a hierarchy to limit what the players can do. They use their skills wherever they can make a difference.

Life at Valve

Valve does not reveal its profitability but co-founder and managing director Gabe Newell, is supposedly one of the richest people on the planet. Apart from its success, Valve is also known as one of the best examples of a large organization that operates a flat organizational structure.

Every employee is encouraged to be active and assume many roles. The following are extracts from the Valve Handbook for New Employees, which highlights that encouragement:[1]

> 'We want innovators, and that means maintaining an environment where they'll flourish. That's why Valve is flat. It's our shorthand way of saying that we don't have any management, and nobody "reports to" anybody else. We do have a founder/president, but even he isn't your manager. This company is yours to steer—toward opportunities and away from risks. You have the power to green-light projects. You have the power to ship products.'

> 'There's no red tape stopping you from figuring out for yourself what our customers want, and then giving it to them.'

'We've heard that other companies have people allocate a percentage of their time to self-directed projects. At Valve, that percentage is 100. Since Valve is flat, people don't join projects because they're told to. Instead, you'll decide what to work on.'

'Deciding what to work on can be the hardest part of your job at Valve. This is because, as you've found out by now, you were not hired to fill a specific job description. You were hired to constantly be looking around for the most valuable work you could be doing.'

Roles at Valve are fluid. No one has a title. Employees are active in taking on roles that suit the work needed by the organization. Look at the credits Valve puts in their games—there are no titles, just a list of names in alphabetical order.

Flatter not flat

Organizations like Valve have started out flat and scaled accordingly. For large organizations with entrenched hierarchy, becoming totally flat may not be realistic. However, a flatter structure is possible. Some form of hierarchy may exist but flattening the hierarchy to reduce the bureaucracy is crucial.

In order to have a flatter structure, organizations need to have a platform on which employees can communicate and collaborate. They must be able to do this, at any time, from anywhere, and on a mobile device of their choice.

Leaders have to be servant leaders. In a hierarchy, power and authority are located at the top of the pyramid. When the servant-leader power is shared, the needs of others are paramount, and help is given to enable employees to develop and perform at their peak. Servant leadership turns the power pyramid upside down: instead of employees working to serve the leader, the leader exists to serve the employees.

Employees have to be given autonomy and self-management. This is a considerable mindset shift and will require a rigorous effort throughout the organization to accept the change and truly embrace it. Authority has to be delegated to allow employees to be active and engage in activities that fulfill their needs as well as those of the whole organization.

Game score

We need to encourage active participation of employees throughout the organization. The structure needs to be as innovative as the products and services the organization produces. If employees believe they can add value, they need to be able to apply that value actively wherever it is needed in the organization and not be constrained by organizational hierarchy.

On and off the soccer pitch, soccer players are able to participate in a wide range of activities. Their ideas, when planning game tactics and reviewing played matches, are heard and considered. They know that they can share ideas openly and everyone will listen. This increases the interchange, and innovation and creativity on and off the pitch. Players are active participants.

Span of control

'Span of control' was originally a military term that referenced the number of subordinates that directly report to a particular manager. Flat organizations have a 'wide' span of control and tall organizations have a 'narrow' span of control.

The key consideration should be a structure that suits the organization (its customer and markets) and matches the capability of its employees.

If an organization were to flatten its structure, it would appear that a manager's span of control would increase to a point where he/she would have too many people to 'manage', and the workload would become too high. However, the opposite is actually the case.

The soccer manager has a wide span of control but this doesn't increase his or her workload. Managing three players as opposed to 30 players doesn't increase the workload when the players themselves are responsible for forging relationships, teamwork, practice, exercise, and support. They are allowed to self-manage.

How it works

Genuine flat structures have a self-managing workforce. Employees have delegated decision-making authority, autonomy, and empowerment, and red tape is eliminated.

Therefore, the 'manager' has less to do. The planning, coordinating, controlling, staffing, and directing activities of a manager in a tall structure are pushed out to all employees (rather than just a select few).

Management is not the right of a few but the responsibility of everyone.

Employees in an authentic flat structure are responsible for forging relationships, planning their work, coordinating and collaborating with others, acquiring resources to undertake their work, and for making decisions as needed.

Good morning

Morning Star has adhered to a flat structure since it was founded in 1970. Albeit being 'born flat', Morning Star has many successes that an existing hierarchical organization can learn from when considering flattening its structure.

An extract from the Morning Star Self-Management Institute explains what self-management means:[1]

> *'Individual Colleagues, directed by their Personal Commercial Mission, are principally responsible for organizing their relationships. Their Personal Commercial Mission is their 'boss.' The managerial functions of*

planning, organizing, staffing, directing, and controlling are the personal responsibility of each Colleague.

Self-Management is an alternative to the traditional, hierarchical method of organizing we see most often in modern organizations.'

Self-management

It is important to note that self-management is a mind shift. It is more than just *talking* about autonomy, empowerment, delegation etc. It is also about recognizing that employees are the people with the greatest insight into the management of their day-to-day functions and are in the best position to take immediate action when circumstances demand a response or a change in course. Actions and decisions are not randomly given to a select few who we call 'managers'.

Game score

Flattening the hierarchy will reduce the number of managers and increase their span of control without increasing their workload.

Self-management should be implemented to the point it allows decision-making to be made by those in the best position. It should give employees autonomy to 'get the job done' while following the organizational principles or operating within specified 'guardrails'.

When employees truly take ownership of outcomes, they are empowered to make a difference, innovate, and be creative.

Soccer players are best placed to make decisions when the game is in play. The managers and coaches allow them independence of thought, decision-making, and response.

Managers and coaches know that they cannot control the game from the sidelines and have to let go. The players know more about what is happening on the field than the coach or manager and, therefore, are best placed to manage the situation as they see fit.

CHAPTER 13

De-label

In traditional hierarchical organizations, titles are very important. They are a sign of past performance, power, and prestige.

On the winning soccer team, the right to contribute and be heard does not come with the title of manager, coach, captain, or striker. It would not be a winning team if only the captain could contribute to the planning for the next game. In many soccer teams, roles are also fluid: we can have player-coach and player-manager and manager-coach. One of the best players Liverpool FC ever had was Kenny Daglish. He was a player-manager from 1985–1990. He won the *Double* (league title and FA Cup) in his first season as player-manager, and went on to win two more league titles and an FA Cup. There was no conflict in having fluidity of role and changes of title.

Some genuinely flat organizations have done away with roles and titles altogether.

At Morning Star, everyone is known as a 'Colleague'.

At W.L. Gore, everyone is known as an 'Associate'.

At Zappos, everyone is known as a 'Partner'.

But there are various degrees of de-labelling.

Temporary flat hierarchy

When Nate Garvis, author of *Naked Civics*, was VP of Government Affairs at Target, he asked everyone to de-label themselves before beginning a meeting. He would remind everyone to de-label from their roles and titles so that everyone in the meeting no longer had to observe hierarchical rules and that everyone's opinions were of equal value. Garvis flattened the hierarchy for a short period.

CO2 Partners describe Garvis' 4-step process to flatten the hierarchy and the benefits to be gained, as follows:[1]

Step 1: De-label

When you begin your meetings, ask everyone to de-label from their roles. I remember this practice from psychodrama. You actually state, 'I am not the VP of manufacturing' (or whatever your title is at the time). With a crew the size of the one Garvis led, this would be too cumbersome, so he would simply remind all participants to de-label from their titles and roles. To him, this meant no one had to observe hierarchical rules, and everyone's opinions carried equal weight. He said it takes a while for a team to get accustomed to interacting without their titles mattering.

Step 2: Give a piece of yourself

Before diving headlong into the meeting, Garvis would ask people to share something personal about themselves so that the team could see beyond the hierarchy. They would begin to see each other as people.

Step 3: Critical feedback

Garvis is extremely right-brained and probably generated an infinite number of great ideas for his team, but he knows that great ideas aren't enough. They must be challenged and fully accepted. In a hierarchical structure like Target, it is very difficult to challenge your boss's ideas. *Flattening a hierarchy* allows critical feedback to happen. When everyone has de-labelled, they can say what they really think. Ideas get fire-tested, and acceptance is earned.

At first 'strategic inefficiency' did not go well, so Garvis amped up the message with incentives to teammates who did the best job of challenging his ideas. The one with the best critique got a prize. As soon as they could see he was serious about this feedback, they saw it was safe to provide the same feedback to one another. This dramatically changed the culture of his department.

Step 4: Re-label

Once critical feedback has been given and rewarded, it's time to re-label. With hierarchical titles and roles re-established, work can be done efficiently through familiar and prescribed channels.

Neither entitled or titled

Neither entitled or titled is the title of an article about Gusto—an organization that has no titles. The LinkedIn article by Jessica Yuen describes how the Gusto leadership team decided to get rid of titles altogether and despite being prepared for an employee backlash, they found the move was welcomed with open arms.[2]

Yuen acknowledges that while the decision to have no titles makes sense today, the option is open to be revisited in the future as the organization evolves.

Once the titles were removed, job applications were received by people who would never before have thought to apply.

'During the research phase, many companies had mentioned that they felt like they were attracting the wrong kinds of candidates when they had titles. By not having them in the first place, you can filter those people out. That was a really fascinating premise for us to explore. If we're truly a "no-egos" culture, we can zero in on the people who are more likely to thrive here. Fewer candidates are coming through, but we're talking to more people who are better aligned.'

Gusto have found that 'no titles' supports their goal of #OneTeamOneDream

Holacracy

It would be remiss of me in a chapter about no titles and de-labelling not to mention holacracy. Holacracy was famously adopted by Zappos and Medium and has received a mass of mixed press about the success of adoption. Holacracy has been misrepresented as the system that has no managers, no hierarchy, no titles etc.

Holacracy, the brainchild of Brian J. Robertson, maintains a hierarchy but moves power from individuals in a hierarchical pyramid down into circles. Each employee has a role instead of a job title. Within the circles, the roles are regularly reviewed and transferred.

Decision-making is placed where is should be—entirely with each circle. Rather than managers and direct reports, there are 'lead-links' who oversee the circles or projects that need 'roles' to be filled.

CEO Tony Hsieh announced, in late 2013, that his online shoe retailer Zappos would be getting rid of traditional manager roles and adopting holacracy. The media went into a frenzy of criticism. This got worse when Hsieh believed that things were moving too slowly and asked staff to get on board or take a severance pay. The media chose to focus on the 18% who took the payout, and not the 82% who remained.

Despite adverse press, Hsieh is continuing with the adoption of holacracy at Zappos where employees act more like entrepreneurs and seek multiple roles. (Employees lower down in the organization can have a great impact.)

Amazon acquired Zappos in 2009 in a deal valued at $1.2 billion. Hsieh has remained at the helm. It continues to be acclaimed in the press for its exceptionally high levels of customer service and is praised ad infinitum as one of the best places to work.

Zappos has great employee engagement and retention across its 1,500 employees, and 2016 was Zappos' lowest turnover rate since its founding more than 18 years ago.

I think Tony, as all of his 'partners' (employees) call him, is doing something right. Zappos is a leading 21st century organization to which we can all aspire.

Game score

We have to move away from decision-making based on position in the hierarchy. Whether we get rid of job titles altogether and aspire to be a Gusto, Morning Star or W.L. Gore or take a more tempered approach like that of Garvis, de-labelling has value to enable decentralized decision-making, increased collaboration and contribution, and self-management.

We have to flatten the hierarchy and move away from an organization in which direction is determined by position to one in which authority is pushed down to where it makes most sense to reside. Management exists to support employees and not the other way around.

If the organization is going to survive in a world of constant and complex change, power has to be distributed and not retained by a designated few.

In soccer, the captain cannot make all the decisions. Authority to make decisions and take action must be pushed out to the entire team. The role of the manager and the coach is to support the players and not make all the decisions. The game is played on a level playing field where everyone has the same opportunity.

CHAPTER 14

Fast to change direction

Flatter structures work well for organizations that need to innovate and respond quickly in a rapidly changing environment. Large organizations with traditional hierarchies and a command and control management approach have to flatten the hierarchy and operate more like a smaller organization unless they want to be adversely disrupted.

Organizations no longer have the luxury of watching and waiting to see what the competition is going to do and then react accordingly. Organizations have to change direction fast and respond to signals in order to stay ahead of the competition.

Soccer teams have to be continually ahead of the game and ready to change direction. The game has dramatically changed over the last decade with increased player fitness and increased intensity of activities.

Scientific research in 2016 revealed that the amount of sprinting in the English Premier League has increased by 50% in ten years. The analysis of 473 Premier League players showed that the high intensity sprints came at a price: after just a couple of minutes of sprinting, players had a hard time keeping up with the game for upwards of five minutes.

Data, such as this, means that managers and coaches have to take an immediate and hard look at training methods and techniques and be prepared to change direction quickly. Just like an organization, they have to adapt quicker and more aggressively to retain a winning position.

Walmart shifts

In September 2017, Walmart announced a change in its structure in order to improve communication and execution, streamline decision-making, and accelerate its pace of change. Walmart reduced its six US divisional groups to four and 44 regional groups to 36. The restructure was in direct response to increased competition from the likes of Amazon and other grocers who were all jostling to take Walmart's top spot in the market.

Spokesman Kory Lundberg told Supermarket News in an email:[1]

'As retail and the customer are changing, we're putting people who are equipped to run great stores and understand, embrace and execute change at an unprecedented rate in the right roles and in the right locations.'

CEO Doug McMillon is quoted as saying:

'Retail is constantly evolving, and it's critical that we move even faster as the customer and competitive landscape continue to change.'

Rapid response to market change

When change is constant, the biggest challenge facing organizations is being able to respond rapidly to changes driven by competition, consumers, market conditions, and emerging technology.

The only way organizations will be able to respond faster to change will be through a flatter hierarchical structure and removal of the unnecessary bureaucracy it brings.

Organizational change management's overarching priority should be to ensure that everyone in the organization is resilient, agile, and able to adapt. We need to create an organization in which everyone leads. We have to realize that we can no longer predict what is around the corner, and we have to be prepared to change direction rapidly when needed.

Fast growth by fast change

Corporate Travel Management Solutions (CTMS) has grown rapidly over the last 20 years. CEO, Tom Osovitzki, attributes this to the CTMS flat structure. CTMS has 160 employees and seven global offices but has only two levels of management, including the C-suite.[2]

At CTMS, issues get resolved in minutes not days. The flat hierarchy means that the organization, and others like it, is faster, more agile, and more innovative. It can change direction faster because employees are empowered to use their own knowledge to solve issues, make decisions, and innovate.

Game score

Organizations are flattening their structures and reducing the hierarchy so they can be fast to change direction. These organizations and their employees accept that change is constant and that responses to changing conditions, whether driven internally or externally, need to be immediate. It is not BAU (business-as-usual) anymore; it's CAU (change-as-usual).

Organizations have to be able to change direction just as fast as the environment around them changes.

Inertia is the enemy and momentum is our new best friend.

It goes without saying that if a soccer team is slow to change direction during a game, it will lose the game. Winning soccer teams are always ready to change direction.

CHAPTER 15

Employee high influence

Morning Star Self-Management Institute:[1]

'It doesn't make a lot of sense to give the decision-making authority to the person that is furthest (literally) away from the actual work being done.'

Past W.L. Gore CEO Terri Kelly:[2]

'It's far better to rely upon a broad base of individuals and leaders who share a common set of values and feel personal ownership for the overall success of the organization. These responsible and empowered individuals will serve as much better watchdogs than any single, dominant leader or bureaucratic structure.'

Both of the above quotes (which I have referenced earlier but are worthy of repetition), demonstrate the reason organizations need to give employees increased influence which is enabled via a flat or flatter organizational structure.

Everyone on the soccer team, regardless of what role they play, needs to be able to influence if the team is to win. Giacinto Facchetti was an Italian defender. He was regarded as being the first fullback capable of making bursting runs down the flank and contributing to the attack without ignoring his defensive responsibilities. He was able to influence through contribution to the attack even though he was a fullback.

Franz Beckenbauer, a FIFA World Cup winner for Bayern Munich, influenced the way the sweeper role was played. He changed the role to one of an attacking, creative sweeper though his ability to read the game, and defend from behind the center-backs while also being 'attack minded' as the team progressed up the field. His position as sweeper did not limit his ability to influence.

Lev Yashin was a goalkeeper for the old Soviet Union during the 1950s and 60s. He make 75 appearances for the national team and played his entire club career with Dynamo Moscow. He embraced the idea that his role was not just about making saves from shots. He dominated the entire penalty area and defensive zones; he was happy to run out of his goal and actually play as a sweeper. His position as goalkeeper did not stifle his ability to influence as a sweeper.

When Ricardo Semler, CEO of Semco, put the power of influence in the hands of all his employees, he devolved and distributed power. For the past 20 years, leaders from all over the world have flocked to Semco's door to learn from its unconventional approach (nearly 80 universities have published Semco case studies and Semler's own book, *Maverick*, has sold over a million copies).

Self-determination

Research by Deci and Ryan on Self-Determination Theory has revealed that giving employees autonomy and support results in higher job satisfaction and better job performance.[3]

Deci and Ryan (1985, 2000) discovered three core psychological needs of an employee. They are autonomy, competence, and relatedness (the need for social connection and intimacy). Fulfilling these needs leads to autonomous motivation, high-quality performance, and wellness.

Autonomy does not mean to be independent of others but is the need we all have to steer our life in the direction we want. It means we want a sense of freewill when we are doing something.

Competence is the desire to control and master our environment.

Relatedness is our desire to interact with and be connected to others.

This research demonstrates that providing employees with high influence (autonomy and competence) will increase engagement and productivity.

Life at Zappos

Zappos has flattened its hierarchy and has a culture that supports autonomy and competence as well as relatedness.

In 1999, Tony Hsieh became the CEO of Zappos; today, Zappos is a wholly owned subsidiary of Amazon (having been acquired for $1.2 billion in 2009) and its roughly 1,500 employees, head-quartered in Las Vegas, produce in excess of $2 billion in revenues annually.

Hsieh has focused on creating an organizational culture in which customer service representatives have the same level of authority to help customers, as he does. At Zappos, everyone has the responsibility to create WOW. They can influence how customer service is delivered.

Game on at Valve

We have already looked at Valve, which is a smaller organization than Zappos with around 250 employees, but is just as well known for its organizational structure and culture. Valve does not assign managers to permanent positions, but rather has leaders on a project-by-project basis. Employees are not assigned to departments but are allowed to work on whatever project they feel they can contribute to and influence the outcomes.

According to the Valve Handbook for New Employees, Valve is more profitable per employee than Amazon, Microsoft and Google.[4]

The Valve website states:[5]

> *We've been boss-free since 1996.* Imagine working with super smart, super talented colleagues in a free-wheeling, innovative environment—no bosses, no middle management, no bureaucracy. Just highly motivated peers coming together to make cool stuff. It's amazing what creative people can come up with when there's nobody there telling them what to do.'

Also on the Valve website is a list of Valve employees. The list is in alphabetical order, not in order of any seniority. This is the same as the credits on any Valve game.

The following diagram is from the Valve Employee Handbook. It describes how to work without a boss. Essentially the employees can influence the direction of the organization.

Fig. 3-1 **Method to working without a boss**

step 1. Come up with a bright idea
step 2. Tell a coworker about it
step 3. Work on it together
step 4. Ship it!

Source: http://media.steampowered.com/apps/valve/
Valve_NewEmployeeHandbook.pdf

Game score

A flat organization *manages* employees less and gives them increased involvement and influence over the decision-making process. These structures have leaders not managers.

Employees are actively encouraged to influence outcomes and they are motivated to drive organizational success. When employees are able to influence, they have skin in the game.

Soccer players need freedom and autonomy in order to be creative and innovative, and win the game. If players do not have high influence over the way in which the game is played, performance will suffer and games will be lost.

CHAPTER 16

Employee ownership

Whatever position a person plays within an organization, having a sense of ownership results in making decisions with more thought, responsibility, and care. When employees have a sense of ownership, motivation, creativity, and innovation increase. When there is employee ownership, employees will be constantly looking for ways to do things differently and improve.

Managers and coaches work with the entire soccer team to identify the common values, attitudes, and beliefs that the team wants. This collaborative approach provides players with a sense of ownership for the team outcomes.

Employee ownership at Gore

I have talked about W.L. Gore in earlier chapters and have also quoted CEO Terri Kelly talking about employees having personal ownership for the overall success of the organization.

W.L. Gore is known for its flat structure. Although there is a structure (divisions, business units etc.), there is no organizational chart, no hierarchy, and no bosses. Gore's philosophy is that individuals don't need close supervision; they need mentoring and support.

Number 52

Gore has earned a spot on the *Fortune 100 Best Companies to Work For* list every year since 1998, and in 2017 was in the number 52 position.[1]

The fundamental beliefs on the W.L. Gore website epitomize the principles of employee ownership.[2]

> *'We also believe we're all in the same boat. As Associates, we have a vested interest in the success of the company, and we share in Gore's risks and rewards while having an added incentive to stay committed to our enterprise's long-term success. As a result, we feel we're all in this effort together, and believe we should always consider what's best for the enterprise as a whole when making decisions.'*

At Gore, 'Associates' can make decisions, choose the work they do, and make commitments to their colleagues on the outcomes they will achieve. They are encouraged to experiment. As a result, they have a stake in the organizations success and a feeling of ownership.

Benefits

So what benefits do organizations reap when there is a sense of ownership?

When leaders entrust employees with a sense of responsibility and ownership towards their role, it fosters collaboration at work for maximized productivity. When employees have a sense of ownership of their job, they tend to become better performers at work. Higher employee engagement not only leads to increased productivity and profitability but also increased motivation, innovation, and creativity.

Lower turnover reduces the cost of attrition and retains talent.

Engagement and low turnover will also result in the attraction of talent as the organization is seen as a great place to work.

High performing organizations have employees who 'own' outcomes. There is a culture of accountability, trust, and mutual respect. Employees treat the business as if it were their own. They handle actions and decisions with due care and attention. Ownership is about taking initiative and doing the right thing for the business.

When there is a sense of ownership employees are aligned to the values and culture of the organization, and identify with the goals and objectives.

As in the Gore example, there is a sense of 'we are all in this together'.

How to get there

The Gore example and those of other organizations in which employees have a sense of ownership have some basic things in common. They all do the following.

* Actively encourage employee involvement in all aspects of the business.

* Encourage cross team collaboration. Teams are often fluid and their composition changes as employees decide what they want to work on.

* Make it easy for employees to navigate the organization to support collaboration.

- Provide a supportive framework with a culture of reward and recognition.

- Encourage innovation and experimentation with a no-blame culture when things go wrong as long as they were done with the good of the organization in mind.

- Establish common values, which everyone can identify with and live by.

- Create a common sense of purpose.

- Build trust and mutual respect.

- Hold everyone accountable.

- Allow employees to make decisions, initiate, and drive change.

- Allow everyone to challenge the status quo and allow everyone to contribute to discussions in regards to alternative approaches.

- Create continual feedback loops for all parts of the organization—up, down and across. Support this with continual learning and development.

- Give employees flexibility and choices.

- Don't tell employees they are empowered; tell them they already had the power.

- Make sure there are leaders not managers.

- And finally, kill the hierarchy to remove the bureaucracy otherwise we can't do any of the above.

Most of these actions will not happen overnight, but organizations can start to move in the right direction. I suggest looking at some of the organizations that have challenged their status quo to foster employee ownership.

Organizations that aspire to do some, if not all, are leading the way. Organizations like Gore, Valve, Semco, General Electric, Caterpillar, Morning Star, and Pixar.

Number 99

Another organization featured in the *Fortune 100 Best Companies to Work For* list in 2017 was FedEx. It was at position 99.[3]

FedEx gives drivers ownership, which means they are in charge of figuring out the best route to serve their customers most efficiently. No one tells them how to do their job; they simply need to achieve their goal: get their deliveries to the right people quickly.

Tom Peters, the management guru, has made the story about a FedEx employee and a helicopter a legend in demonstrating what can happen when employees feel 'ownership'. The story goes that back in the 1980s, a blizzard in California took down a telephone tower located in the mountains that served the main FedEx call center. The phone company was unable to get to the top of the mountain to repair it.

A 'regular' FedEx employee worked out that he had the ability to fix the failure. He rented a helicopter (paid for with his own credit card) and flew to the top of the mountain where he fixed the tower. In so doing, the FedEx call center want back online.

The crux of the story was that the FedEx employee felt he had 'ownership' of the problem but also of the outcome.

It is also important to note that the employee was empowered and felt he could make the decision. It did not have to go up and down a hierarchy of control, which would have led either to total inertia or to a considerable and unnecessary delay in restoring call center operations.

Game score

When employees have a sense of ownership, they are motivated, innovative, and creative. Employee engagement increases, which leads to increased productivity, which in turn has a positive effect on the bottom line. Profitability goes up.

A sense of ownership is one of the most powerful advantages a soccer team can have. Players are loyal, and their output and effort will increase. They will consistently lift their game.

Managers and coaches spread that sense of ownership throughout the team. They give the players responsibility for the outcomes of a game and engage them in collaborative decision-making.

CHAPTER 17

High collaboration

Structure can hamper collaboration. In a hierarchical organization, employees tend not to be engaged or committed to the work they do. There is limited collaboration.

More organizations are recognizing that their structure is hampering effective collaboration. Hierarchical and siloed structures obstruct cross-functional working, collective problem solving, and effective communication that supports dynamic collaboration.

The level of autonomy and collaboration within the workforce is determined by the organizational structure. Therefore, it is critical that organizations not only realize this but also take constructive actions to break down the hierarchy.

Soccer teams are built to perform effectively under constantly changing conditions. The winning teams succeed because they have a collaborative mindset. They know that there is interdependency between all the players on the field. Winning teams play in a highly collaborative manner. Without collaboration, there is not an opportunity to tap into the talent on the team.

Organizations don't have to be a flat structure like a W.L. Gore, Zappos, Valve, Basecamp (formerly 37signals) or Pixar but they do need to be moving in that direction. These organizations have structures that foster high levels of collaboration.

What is collaboration?

Collaboration is not just another word for teamwork. Teamwork is when two or more people come together to complete a task. Collaboration is teamwork with these attributes.

Brainstorming: 'Putting our heads together' to challenge the status quo, and offer alternative thoughts and ideas. Teams can be given a pre-defined solution to deliver. When teams brainstorm, they can challenge the pre-defined solution and instead address the problem or opportunity that needs to be solved. The outcome may be very different when employees collaborate rather than engage in just teamwork. Collaboration means active interaction and debate.

De-label: This means 'leave your title at the door'. When we truly collaborate, everyone is equal. Ideas are encouraged from everyone regardless of their position within the organization. Titles do not mean your ideas are considered less worthy of discussion or more important. Trust and respect are the foundations for effective collaboration.

Shared sense of purpose: When employees truly collaborate, they see the value of working together. Working together is not forced upon them. They collaborate willingly and gladly. They see the benefit of collaboration not only for themselves but also for the organization as a whole.

Benefits

So why do we need high levels of collaboration? There are many benefits arising from high-levels of collaboration.

They include increased:

- Employee engagement
- Agility (quick to respond)
- Fluidity (quick to change direction)
- Productivity
- Employee retention
- Competitive advantage
- Profitability
- Employee well-being
- Speed to market
- Motivation.

Every organization that wants to survive and thrive in a world of rapid and disruptive change, needs to acquire these outcomes. Collaboration will bring these benefits.

Wirearchy

An organizational structure model, with connection and collaboration at its core, is wirearchy. In 2015, Jon Husband, compiled the book *Wirearchy: Sketches for the Future of Work*. The book has many contributors who propose that Wirearchy is the alternative to hierarchy if we want to meet the needs of our world today.

Jon defines Wirearchy as follows:[1]

'Wirearchy is about the power and effectiveness of people working together through <u>connection and collaboration</u>, taking responsibility individually and collectively rather than relying on traditional hierarchical status.

Wirearchy is an emergent organizing principle that informs the ways that purposeful human activities and the structures in which they are contained are evolving from top-down direction and supervision (hierarchy's command and control) to champion-and-channel. That is, the championing of ideas and innovation, and the channeling of time, energy, authority, and resources to testing those ideas and the possibilities for innovation they carry.'

I do not profess to be an expert in organizational design but I suspect, as with any model, that it could work for some and not for others. However, there are elements of the model that underpin effective collaboration that should be afforded attention.

The are four core elements to Wirearchy that do just that: knowledge, trust, credibility, and a focus on results.

So what would someone need to do in a Wirearchy organization?

As a *leader,* be prepared to listen deeply, be responsible, be accountable, and be transparent.

As a *manager,* learn how to be an effective listener and coach.

As an *employee,* develop a clear understanding of how to be empowered, valuable, and of service.

What I liked about Wirearchy is that:

a. It supports the notion that a hierarchical structure will not support an organization looking to thrive in today's disruptive world. To quote Jon: *'One thing now seems clear. Adapt now or adapt later, but adapt you will have to.'*

b. It stresses the need for people to connect and <u>collaborate</u> in order to innovate. Innovation is key to organizational success.

c. It is about letting people get on with achieving outcomes in their own way, which will surface new ways of addressing problems, issues, and opportunities.

d. It talks about the *'furthest possible distribution of all authority',* which to me, means autonomy and distributed decision-making—an organization where everyone can initiate and drive change.

e. It acknowledges we need both <u>collaboration</u> and cooperation if we want to generate social and economic value.

f. It emphasizes the need for active listening, accountability, transparency, and empowerment.

All of these attributes are fundamental in my *Kill the Hierarchy Model.* It doesn't matter whether an organization aspires to Wirearchy or Holacracy, it is a shift that is needed to remove the inertia that comes with hierarchy. In a world of rapid and constant change, inertia is your enemy,

Remember, one model does not fit all, so select the parts from all the models available that will enable the organization to become responsive to rapid change and cultivate an environment of collaboration.

Game score

Collaboration is not new but it's also not commonly used organization-wide nor adopted as a shared and collective way of working. It is often seen as a one-off activity.

Organizations with high levels of collaboration will reap the benefits discussed here. Those that don't will lag behind, lose business, and be unable to attract the talent they need.

I trust that everyone would agree that a winning team needs everyone to be a team player. The soccer team will not win if players are playing the game as individuals. They win because they collaborate both on and off the field.

Managers and coaches ensure the players have the necessary skills to collaborate effectively knowing that they will outperform teams that don't.

CHAPTER 18

Everyone leads

When everyone leads employees know they are making a difference and getting things done. They are motivated and engaged. Organizations must give employees autonomy to lead. This needs trust and commitment. It also means breaking down the hierarchy so everyone can make decisions, and initiate and drive change.

There may be principles to guide employees or guardrails within which they can operate, but everyone is encouraged to lead to the extent that makes good sense for the organization. When everyone leads, they are held accountable for their actions and there is a no-blame culture. When everyone leads, it doesn't mean that there is absolutely no structure. When teams self-manage there can still be a team leader, but that role can also rotate around the team on a regular basis.

On the soccer field, as in the organization, leadership does not equate to taking charge. On a winning team, everyone can lead. Influence, authority, and the ability to lead can come from any player, on and off the field. Managers and coaches encourage the players to seize opportunities for leadership, and when they do, both the team and the player achieve more.

The need for a flat(ter) structure

We can only have an organization where everyone leads when we have a flat or flatter structure. In a hierarchical structure with a command and control approach to management, employees will not lead. They will wait to be told what to do, and all decision-making will be held by a few and directed to many.

Employees will not put their head above the parapet to make a suggestion or share an idea, due to the fear of being shot down. Employees will not initiate change, even if they are best placed to do so, because that's not their job. In a hierarchical structure, change is driven by those with titles that suggest they should know what they are doing.

Innovation and creativity will be stifled. The organization will be slow to make decisions, and unable to respond to internal and external forces requiring an imminent or immediate response.

Employee engagement will be low, attrition will be high, and it will be hard to attract talent. Millennials will not be attracted to an organization with a hierarchical structure. Millennials have a lot to say and want to be heard. They want to make a difference.

In terms of working for an organization, millennials are looking for:

- An opportunity to learn and grow
- An interest in the type of work
- An organization that encourages creativity
- An organization that is a fun place to work
- An informal work environment.

Hierarchical organizations just won't cut it. Organizations have to look at their structure and ways in which to flatten them— now. Talent is attracted to organizations in which everyone can genuinely lead and make a difference.

Size doesn't matter

Google, despite its mammoth size, has a flat structure, with few levels of middle management. Every employee can lead. Google's policy of empowering and facilitating employees' work has led to a large number of innovations and, consequently, to the outstanding success of the company.

Eric Schmidt was CEO of Google from 2001 to 2011. Two of his leadership principles were:

- Let your employees own the problems you want them to solve.

- Allow employees to function outside the company hierarchy.

To make employees own their work, Schmidt provided a very broad definition of the company goal and left the implementation entirely to the employees. He defined Google's goal as 'Organizing the world's information and making it universally accessible and useful.'

Every employee could relate to it and lead to achieve it. Schmidt did not allow hierarchy to obstruct employee performance, and allowed them freedom to create their own projects and choose their own teams. They were allowed to lead.

Game score

When organizations nurture leadership on an organization-wide level, the entire organization and every employee will prosper and grow.

Everyone has a significant contribution to make and their voices need to be heard.

Moreover, they need to be able to challenge the status quo, make decisions, initiate and drive change and be seen as leaders in their own right.

Leadership in the soccer team is distributed. In some moves, some players take control, and in other moves, others take the lead. Leadership is fluid and dispersed. The best players know when to lead and when not to. They know when it is best to lead and when to follow.

Apart from at half time, the soccer game is 90 minutes of rapid play. There is no time for the team to come together and decide who is playing in what position. This means that everyone on the team knows their play and what they need to do at any point to bring the game home. Organizations today have to be the same.

CHAPTER 19

Open communication

Communication is the flow of information between people.

Organizations will not survive without it. Open communication occurs when everyone can participate, discuss, debate, and express ideas.

Organizations will not thrive without it. Everyone is equal and participating on a level playing field with a transparent relationship.

In a dynamic game like soccer, which is constantly changing with every move, open and effective communication can be the difference between turning a possession into a goal scored or a goal conceded. Open communication in soccer provides the players with invaluable information for making the best decisions both on and off the ball.

Just like in soccer, open communication in the workplace will increase employee performance, engagement, and motivation. Increased productivity increases profitability. There is a financial and reputational motive to create a culture of open communication.

Open communication can only effectively flow when the hierarchy is flattened. If communication has to go from one level of authority to another for approval before it gets disseminated, it will have changed in nature (content) and be received too late by its recipients. It would be like Chinese whispers in slow motion.

A flat organizational structure with reduced management layers means the CEO can have direct communication with virtually all employees, which promotes a free flow of ideas and information.

Benefits

Employee engagement

Open and transparent communication gives everyone visibility of where the organization is going and what needs to be done to get it there. There is a shared sense of purpose and everyone is working towards the same outcome. This increases morale, motivation, and engagement.

Employee attraction and retention

Open communication leads to employee engagement, which in turn means that organizations can both retain and attract the talent that they need.

As Steve Jobs is often quoted as saying:

'If you want to hire great people and have them stay working for you, you have to let them make a lot of decisions and you have to be run by ideas, not hierarchy. The best ideas have to win, otherwise good people don't stay.'

Rapid feedback loops

Open communication allows for rapid feedback loops where communication flows freely up and down (as well as across) the organization.

Feedback lies at the heart of open communication. Feedback loops increase competitiveness.

When all levels of the organization can provide feedback on decisions, problems, opportunities, work-in-progress etc. the organization can be driven in the right direction. Feedback can be received from the place in which it has greater context. Employees on the front line can provide real-time feedback in regards to the customer experience, which could result in change being made to service offerings or service delivery. A person in marketing, who becomes aware of a planned market push by a competitor for a particular product, can provide feedback so that the organization can shift and remain competitive.

Rapid decision-making resulting in successful outcomes is driven by real-time open communication. Open communication and feedback loops are also important to provide employees and their leaders/managers with feedback on performance. The dreaded performance review should not be a bi-yearly or annual event. It should happen all of the time.

For open communication and feedback loops to be effective, trust and respect are paramount.

Clear messages

Open communication provides clarity of the message. The message is not created and then modified numerous times by management who believe they understand the intended audience better than anyone else.

Continual modification muddies the water and clarity is lost. Also, if messages are disseminated through various chains-of-command, they are also subject to variation along the way. By the time they are received by employees, there are various versions of what was intended as one message. Employees receive mixed messages.

Confusion results in employee disengagement and lost productivity while they worry and try to determine what is actually being said.

How to get there

Trust

Number one is trust. An environment of trust can take time to cultivate but without it, communication will not be open and transparent.

All employees (top to bottom) establish trust by making commitments and delivering on them. It is about everyone making themselves vulnerable with each other and knowing that someone has your back.

Platform

Provide a platform for open communications, which could be utilized globally if needed. There are numerous software solutions available to support open communication and sharing of ideas but don't forget to make the selection open too. Involve employees in the selection process, allow them to give feedback and contribute their selection criteria. Involve them in prototyping and pilots. Involve them in shortlisting and final selection.

No blame

No communication, suggestion, idea or feedback should be reproached. If an employee gets slapped down by another employee because their idea is perceived as worthless, they will stop communicating.

Every piece of communication should be openly and enthusiastically welcomed. Don't shoot the messenger.

Handle conflict

Where conflict arises, ensure it gets nipped in the bud; do not allow it to fester. Have a process and facilitation capability in place to address this. Encourage the employee to deal directly with those with whom they have conflict so that the idea of 'open' communication permeates.

Respond

Remember that communication is two-way and that when a response is expected, one should be received. If employees believe that communication is one-way and despite them being heard no corresponding action is being taken, they will stop communicating. They will just say 'what is the point, they are not listening.'

Game score

A flat organizational structure, with fewer layers of management, improves communication. Communication is open, faster, easier, and less likely to be misunderstood or misinterpreted.

Organizations are able to respond faster to feedback and remain competitive.

Effective open communication ensures that everyone is on the same page. When information is being shared efficiently, resilience to a rapidly changing and increasingly complex work environment can be boosted.

Soccer teams win when there is open and effective communication on and off the field.

On the field, we will hear shouts of 'turn', 'man on', 'keeper', 'cross' or 'square'. These are just some examples of widely understood communication that takes place during the game. They form quick and concise communications that relay accurate information to other players.

In a game that is fast, intense, and constantly changing, open, clear, and concise communication is essential for victory. Open communication can be the difference between a win and a defeat. Players need to be provided with accurate information in a timely manner in order to make the best split second decisions they can, both on and off the ball.

CHAPTER 20

Autonomy

Without autonomy, employees become robots moving around aimlessly waiting to be told what to do next. This is not an inspirational, motivational, or engaging place to be for anyone.

Soccer players on a winning team need three things: autonomy (a sense of control and self-management), competence (capability, skill, and ability), and relatedness (a sense of purpose and belonging).

When the game starts, the manager and coach get out of the way and let the game play out. Players have the autonomy to play the game as they see best, given the rapidly changing conditions on the field. They can make decisions and change direction at any time without recourse to a manager or coach. This results in an inspired, motivated, innovative, creative, and winning team.

So what is autonomy?

Autonomy is about giving employees the right to do the work they want, how they want, and when they want. It's about management getting out of the way and letting employees get on with their job.

Autonomy could be choosing which projects to work on, who to work with, when to work and how to get the job done. In an organization with employee autonomy, the focus is on what gets done (outcomes) as opposed to how it gets done.

Autonomy is directly linked to employee engagement and motivation. It increases feelings of ownership and loyalty. This means that talent is both retained and attracted. Increased employee engagement leads to increased productivity and profitability.

Autonomy can also be applied to teams. An autonomous team is one that is self-managing with little or no direction from a manager. When team members work well together, they can build on each other's strengths, and can compensate for other's weaknesses.

This sort of environment has a direct impact on increasing job satisfaction. However, autonomy does not mean that there is outright anarchy.

Guardrails

Organizations have principles or guardrails. The guardrails are like lines on the road that help keep drivers safe and keep them on the road. Guardrails keep everyone aligned to the organization's goals and objectives. They are the parameters within which employees can operate without unnecessary interference.

The US military call this 'doctrine': the mechanism for managing the fog of war and pushing decision-making closer to the ground while providing the lines to guide decision-making and action.

At Gumroad, the successful platform that enables creators to sell products directly to consumers, a focus on a bias towards action, ownership, and a flat organization, is baked into each of its core values (principles).

The Mission & Values website list these values:[1]

Move fast

Move quickly. Do not lag. Once a decision is made, execute it as fast as possible. Ship quickly. Save words. Instead, implement and measure. Perfect is the enemy of good.

Change

Get comfortable with being uncomfortable. Nothing is sacred; everything is in a state of change. As individuals, we should look to place ourselves in a position where we are learning and getting better every day.

Align yourself

Constantly put yourself in a place where the best thing for you is the best thing for everyone with whom you work.

Be open and transparent

Simplify your relationships. Lose the filter. Talk openly about what you care about and the problems with which you are dealing. Get feedback to get better.

Stay focused

Is the thing you are working on right now the most valuable thing you could be doing? A corollary to this: trust others to execute on their objectives so that you can stay focused on your own.

Smile!

Have fun. Don't regret. Don't think too hard. Be optimistic. Assume the best. Things will work out: how could they not?

If all Gumroad employees follow these principles, the organization is in good hands.

Autonomy and flat structure

About 20% of the world's websites are now on the WordPress platform, making it one of the most important internet companies. Automattic, the firm behind WordPress, employs a couple hundred people, who all work remotely, with a highly autonomous flat management structure.

The successful development platform, GitHub, is another highly successful firm with a similar structure. It has no middle managers, employees are beholden to no one, and are encouraged to define their roles in ways that make sense to them. They have autonomy.

We have already looked at W.L. Gore, where all decision-making across 10,000 employees is done through self-managing teams of 8–12 people. At Morning Star, the world's leading tomato ingredient processor, the notion of empowerment assumes that authority trickles down from above, as and when the powerful see fit. In an organization built on the principles of self-management and autonomy, employees aren't given power by the 'higher-ups'—they simply have it.

The Ritz-Carlton is famous for its high levels of customer satisfaction achieved through its excellent customer service, which is underpinned by employee autonomy. For many years, the Ritz-Carlton has given staff $2,000 of discretion per employee per guest that can be used to solve any customer complaint in the manner the employee feels is appropriate. There is no recourse to a higher authority for approval.

Ritz-Carlton employees are known as the Ladies and Gentlemen of the Ritz and have the autonomy to make decisions, craft special moments, and resolve customer issues.

And of course there is Valve Corporation, one of the best-known examples of a large organization that operates on a flat structure.

And did I mention Google?

Google has one aspirational mission statement:

> 'Organize the world's information and make it universally accessible and useful.'

Google has one goal:

> 'Develop services that improve the lives of as many people as possible. Not just for some. For everyone.'

Employees are trusted and given the autonomy to self-manage and deliver on that mission and goal.

And yes, there are principles (which include guardrails):

1. Innovation comes from anywhere

2. Focus on the user

3. Aim to be ten times better

4. Bet on technical insights

5. Ship and iterate

6. Give employees 20% time

7. Default to open processes

8. Fail well

9. Have a mission that matters.

Think of 'focus on the user, 'ship and iterate' and 'fail well' as guardrails. It is ok to ship early rather than waiting until something is perfect. Customers will help us make it 'better' through their feedback. It is ok to do this, as long as we are focused on the user.

There is no stigma attached to failure. In fact, Google treats failure like a badge of honor. If employees don't fail enough, they are not trying hard enough.

Game score

The companies I have mentioned in here would not be the successes they are without giving employees autonomy.

Autonomy = +choice = +engagement = +retention = +motivation = +innovation = +productivity = +profitability = +++success. Now that's an equation I want.

When its time for the soccer team to get onto the field, the coaches and manager get out of the way and let the players get on with their job. They are given the autonomy to play the game in the way that they see best.

There is a shared purpose and goal to win the game doing whatever it takes. The team focus is on what needs to get done, not how it gets done.

CHAPTER 21

High trust

Everyone's business

The only way a flatter hierarchy with less managerial presence will be successful is if there is an environment of trust and mutual respect. Everyone in the organization has to trust everyone else to do the right thing for their colleagues as well as the organization as a whole.

Every player on a soccer team has to trust that their teammates will do their part and will assist in winning the game. Trust allows each player to depend heavily on one another. Good teamwork depends on trust. All of the players need to trust each other. When there is no trust, and the players play as individuals, the whole team is diminished.

Managers and coaches have to win the trust of each other and the players. Without trust, it is impossible to develop individual players and to develop a winning team. Winning trust involves coaching, caring, being transparent, providing feedback, and communicating effectively.

Establishing trust

Sense of purpose

Organizations have to recognize the purpose of the organization. What is it trying to achieve and why? What are the core values that will inspire everyone in the organization so that everyone is working towards a common goal?

Everyone at Google has a shared purpose: to support the mission and achieve the goal. They are unified, and this unity and the sense of purpose inspires trust in everyone in the organization.

When we share a common goal and have a collective sense of purpose, high levels of trust are an outcome. If we believe others have different agendas that don't support the common goal, then mistrust and suspicion permeates the organization and everyone spends time watching their own back.

Walk the talk

We always say that we expect leaders to walk the talk and lead by example, but I think it goes beyond just those in senior positions within the organization.

I think we should expect everyone to walk the talk and lead by example, and when they don't, we should call them on it. In an organization where we want everyone to 'lead', we should hold everyone accountable to serve the purpose of the organization. Leaders respect employees and vice versa. To be respected, we have to respect.

While everyone should lead by example, the charge has to be led by the CEO or the 'owner' of the organization. Everything he or she commits to doing must be done if respect and trust are to be established. If that commitment has to be changed, then transparency and honesty are crucial if respect and trust are to be maintained.

Teams

Research indicates that our ability to maintain close trusting relationships with family, friends, and work colleagues is constrained to probably around 150 people. Of course, we can know more than 150 people at any one time, but it is hard to develop close bonds of trust based on actual experiences with each of them.

W. L. Gore has this approach. Gore doesn't allow a facility to grow to more than 200 people. The belief is that once a unit reaches a certain size, 'we decided' becomes 'they decided.'

The Gore website states:[1]

> *'We believe in the individual and each Associate's potential to help Gore grow and succeed. We also believe in the power of small teams, and through Gore's lattice structure, Associates can communicate freely to assemble talents and diverse perspectives to quickly make good decisions and produce quality work that helps us deliver on our promise to our customers.'*

When teams become too big, 'they decided' dissolves trust.

Enablement

Trust is demonstrated when organizations enable employees to get on with their job.

Many would call this empowerment, but empowerment infers that power is passed down from on high. In a flatter organizational structure, employees always have that power.

Empowerment sounds like power being bestowed by a manager saying, *'I can grant you some power because I am the one who holds all the power.'*

Enablement, empowerment, permission, whatever we want to call it, is critical. Hierarchies with a command and control managerial approach kill trust. It is driven by rules and structures to enforce those rules. We need to trust our employees and not the instruction book.

Transparency

If we are not transparent and hide things from others, there will be no trust. Transparency also enables empowerment.

Sure, some things at certain times cannot be widely shared but this should be the exception. When people perceive that they are not being told the truth, trust will rapidly disappear. Remember that once trust is broken, it will be considerably harder to get it back.

Communication needs to be transparent and honest too. People will see 'spin' when it happens, and once again trust is lost. Telling the truth, albeit sometimes hard, fosters trust and mutual respect.

Everyone is equal

Trust is soon lost when there is the perception that some people are treated more favorably than others. The perception that some are more equal than others will cause trust to quickly diminish.

The good thing about transparency is that it exposes unfairness, and corrective action can be taken quickly. This equality is reflected by the removal of titles in organizations as mentioned earlier. At Morning Star, everyone is a Colleague; at W.L. Gore everyone is an 'Associate'; and in organizations adopting Holacracy, everyone is a 'Partner'. All of these organizations have a flat structure.

Game score

Trust is key to providing employees with autonomy, allowing them to be self-managing, and distributing decision-making.

Treating everyone as equal, being honest and transparent, providing a shared sense of purpose, walking the talk, and creating smaller teams to avoid 'we decided' becoming 'they decided', will foster a sustainable eco-system of trust.

Respect has a ripple effect. When leaders show respect, it can be copied throughout the organization. This cascade of respect will influence how employees treat customers and suppliers.

It is no coincidence that in 2017, Forbes named Costco America's best employer and in the same year, the American Customer Satisfaction (ASCI) Retail Report listed Costco the best department and discount store for customer service.

The players on a winning team have to trust each other. They know that they have an obligation as a true team player to trust and respect their teammates.

Trust is the emotional glue that brings the manager, coach, and players together to create the winning team. There is no place for conflict or disrespect on the team.

CHAPTER 22

Information accessible

Accessible information and knowledge is a key factor in productivity, competitiveness, employee engagement, and growth. It is not enough to make information available; it needs to be accessible by all.

In a flat organization, knowledge and information flows freely, and employees are enabled to make decisions and drive change as they have relevant knowledge and information available to them.

Access to knowledge and information must be easy and intuitive. Accessible information or knowledge sharing in soccer teams can be associated with their sustainability, continuity, and achievement of long-lasting competitive results.

Knowledge sharing can increase the competitive advantage over other teams. It provides an increased capacity for faster decision-making, stimulates innovation and growth, and provides reusable problem solving experiences.

When a player scores a terrific goal, we often refer to them as 'just so talented' or 'only they could pull that off'. What we don't see are the hours of practice that have gone into becoming that talented. *Knowledge* is the journey the soccer star took to get to where they are. It is invaluable information when shared.

When this information is captured and made accessible, the journey can be shared, and a newer player can follow a similar approach to get to a similar level. The information or knowledge can help teammates develop and grow much quicker.

Contribution mindset

Information is only made widely available when everyone in the organization has a contribution mindset. A contribution mindset is required of every employee in a self-managed flatter organization. Employees share information regardless of whether they were asked for it or not. The excuse, 'Well nobody asked me', does not stack up today.

There are systems that will support employees making information available as well as easily accessible by their peers. At Morning Star, employee contribution, whether asked for or not, is written into their Morning Star Colleague Principles.[1]

> *'**Caring and Sharing.** To the degree Colleagues care about themselves, their friends and relatives, fellow Colleagues, suppliers, customers, the environment, the Mission, Principles and facilities, etc., each of us will come closer to achieving our personal goals. In caring for others, each colleague commits to (1) share relevant information with others, (2) take initiative to forward information that they believe may be helpful to another's activities, even if it is not asked for, and (3) responding to respectful inquiries made of them by other Colleagues in a respectful and responsive manner.'*

Knowledge management and organizational structure

When decision-making authority is distributed, the quality of decision-making depends on access to relevant knowledge. To promote knowledge sharing and knowledge exchange, organizations must remove the structural barriers to the interaction of their knowledge workers. They must flatten the hierarchy.

Knowledge management will be impacted by organizational structure. The structure will define how information flows within the organization.

In a hierarchical structure, employees' roles are clearly defined, department composition is relatively static, and there is a clear line of communication etiquette. These organizations constrain the interactions an employee can have and limit knowledge sharing. Flow of information is slow as it moves up and down reporting lines.

In flatter structures, information flows much more freely and knowledge is shared much quicker and broader.

When knowledge management is a source of competitive advantage, organizations have to look at how their structure hinders or promotes the effective knowledge creation, sharing, and utilization. Organizations that adopt flexible and flatter structures, with fewer hierarchical levels, boost the communication, interaction, and knowledge sharing of employees. Interaction is so much easier and unconstricted.

The hierarchical organization reduces the ability of the organization to integrate and share knowledge.

If organizations are going to not only survive but also thrive, the structure needs to enable improved sharing and access to knowledge and information. Hierarchical barriers mean access to information for rapid decision-making is not available.

Employees best situated to make rapid decisions because they have the contextual facts, may not have the additional information or knowledge they need. Therefore, decision-making goes up the chain of command, is centralized, and the organization cannot be responsive to change. Just like dinosaurs unable to respond to change, they will die.

Game score

Knowledge and information is the only sure source of competitive advantage.

Winning organizations are able to consistently create new knowledge, spread it throughout the organization and rapidly manifest it into new technologies and products.

The information or knowledge-based organization has a flat structure, and the knowledge is in the hands of the self-managed workers.

Information on the soccer team has to constantly flow between manager, coach, and player. It has to be updated constantly, as the game has to be adjusted for the team to remain competitive. It has to be accessible to everyone on the team.

Everyone contributes to the collection of knowledge and information that is widely shared across the team.

Principles management

Principles or guardrails help employees make quality decisions faster and with less risk.

Organizations see greater synergy across the organization when employees are provided with context for understanding business needs, guardrails for decision-making support, and responsibility for the decisions they make.

Guardrails are the principles within which employees operate. These principles guide employees and keep everyone aligned.

In soccer, the players also have principles by which they play the game. They have to make instantaneous decisions when faced with rapidly changing conditions but they have principles to guide them.

Principles for the players may include:

- Move into space
- Give the person in possession of the ball passing options
- Anyone can play in any position in order to win the game
- Take initiative and adapt to new and changing conditions

- Keep the game simple

- Everyone must play in the game as a team

- Play to win

At Boeing, there are principles to guide employees in regards to safety. The Boeing safety goal is 'Go for Zero – One Day at a Time'. This means eliminating all workplace injuries and ensuring a safe environment. The principles that guide all employees to achieve this goal are: [1]

- We value human life and well-being above all else and take action accordingly.

- All incidents, injuries, and workplace illnesses are preventable.

- We are personally accountable for our own and collectively responsible for each other's safety.

- By committing to safety first, we advance our goals for quality, cost, and schedule.

Therefore, when making a decision, employees know they are accountable for their own safety and that of others, and human life and well-being take precedence.

Creating guardrails

Guardrails should be agreed upon. The organization could select a representative cross-functional group of employees to define the guardrails and then put them up for comment by the rest of the organization. Once as-near-as-possible-consensus has been achieved, they should be published and subject to regular review based on ongoing feedback.

Guardrails are the guidelines within which employees can act autonomously. They enable employees to make good decisions. Unlike rules, which are constrictive, guardrails allow employees to use their intuition, rational thinking, and their unique contextual understanding of the situation. Focus on the guardrails (principles) not policies.

Guardrails are parameters. Employees need to know the objectives and the associated deadlines. Guardrails give employees the freedom to come up with innovative and creative solutions and ideas.

Just like rules though, guardrails can be broken if an employee believes there is just reason for doing so and no intentional damage to the organization's well-being was intended. In these situations, guardrails should be reviewed and revised as needed.

Fog of war

In the military, 'fog of war' is the term used to describe the uncertainty experienced by soldiers in military operations. The term seeks to encapsulate the uncertainty regarding one's own capability, that of the enemy, and the enemies intent.

The same uncertainly exists in organizations as the 'fog of business.'

The old tools, like long-term planning, do not cut it anymore. They are like headlights that just bounce off the fog. Long-term planning is too rigid and does not allow the organization to respond quickly to rapidly changing environments.

What is needed is guidance for employees to enable rapid decision-making. In addition to the fog lights, there needs to be lines on the road that keep everyone aligned and heading in the same direction.

The Smallest Employee Handbook

Nordstrom is a highly successful American based chain of department stores. The organization has 373 stores operating in 40 US states, Puerto Rico, and Canada and also has an extensive online presence.

Nordstrom is legendary for its employee handbook. It is not a book but a card:

'Welcome to Nordstrom

We're glad to have you with our Company.

Our number one goal is to provide outstanding customer service. Set both your personal and professional goals high.

We have great confidence in your ability to achieve them. Nordstrom Rules.

Rule #1: Use your good judgment in all situations. There will be no additional rules.

Please feel free to ask your department manager, store manager, or division general manager any question at any time.'

In essence, Nordstrom has one principle by which all employees operate, 'Use your good judgment in all situations.'

I would suggest that most organizations would want a little more detail underneath that principle but the Nordstrom intent of principles rather than rules is one to be admired.

Game score

Give employees autonomy and the ability to make rapid-decisions while also giving them the comfort of having guardrails. Guardrails help support employee health and well-being as employees are not stressed about decision-making, which they perceive 'could be above their pay grade'. But it also helps with the health and well-being of the organization as a whole.

Guardrails keeps decision-making aligned with organizational goals and objectives.

The players on the soccer team have to make split-second decisions and have to have autonomy to do so. They have principles or guardrails to guide them.

CHAPTER 24

Leaders coach

Creating a flatter, autonomous work place and allowing employees to self-manage is great. But what if we just let loose and leave everyone to work out what to do and what to work on.

Buffer is an extremely successful social media management solution company. It is also known for its transparency and the way in which it manages its distributed and remote employees. However, Buffer didn't always get it right. When Buffer moved to self-management, it also moved to a completely flat structure. One of the big mistakes it made was removing all 1:1s and mentoring sessions to avoid top down interactions.

This resulted in employees being left to sink or swim, and it was a disaster. So Buffer reintroduced 1:1 coaching sessions. These sessions are a vehicle for working through challenges, and bouncing around worries and concerns with someone who may have been through a similar situation in the past and able offer sound advice.

On a soccer team, coaching sessions are vital. Coaches are about long-term development of the players. They guide the players to reach their full potential. They work with both the individual players and the team. The soccer coach is a mentor, teacher, psychologist, physiologist, and confidante. The leaders in our organizations need to be the same.

It should be noted that someone does not have to possess the title of coach or leader in order to coach. Everyone can coach and everyone can lead.

Any player with diplomacy, facilitation, negotiation, and motivational skills can act as a coach to another player.

Coaching for connectivity

Regular coaching for all employees, including executives, helps connect everyone. Coaching ensures no-one gets left behind. It builds connections between what each person does with the organization's goals and objectives.

Some employees may develop connections on their own while others will require coaching in order to establish connections and maintain them on an ongoing basis.

Employees need to connect to the job and to what is required of them, their leader, their colleagues, and the organization as a whole.

Leaders need to understand the levels of connectivity in each area and work to develop strong connections. Employees will be engaged and motivated as a result.

'I've learned that people will forget what you said, people will forget what you did, but people will never forget how you made them feel.' — Maya Angelou

Coaching sessions

Every leader should help others learn and grow by having resonant coaching sessions.

The following are some of my coaching tips.

Regular sessions

Coaching sessions should be held on a regular basis and not just ad-hoc as time permits. They should only be postponed or rescheduled in extreme circumstances. Regular reschedules or cancellations send messages to employees that, as a coach, you are not serious about their development and well-being, and have higher priorities.

The sessions should also be time-boxed and the employee given all of that time to work with their coach. Coaches cutting sessions short, because they need to do something else, sends the same messages as canceling or rescheduling.

There is no better way to demotivate and disengage employees than when coaches say they are going to give them your time for coaching and then not live up to that commitment. It's your call.

Celebrate achievements

Coaches should start the sessions by celebrating successes and achievements. Take time to reflect on what has been done well before jumping into the next challenge. Employees should be energised and refreshed before the coach dives into the rest of the coaching session.

Listen

Remember, most of the time (around 85% of the session) should be the employee talking—not the coach. The coach listens with a clear and open mind. Be aware that the employee will know when the coach is not in the moment. Coaches need to clear their mind and be present.

Ask

Effective coaches do not give the answers, they ask questions. What the coach would do in a given situation is not necessarily what the employee should do. Employees need to talk about their goals and challenges, and find the answers themselves. Only in this way will the employee be motivated and take ownership of a solution.

Feedback

Coaching sessions are a great vehicle for two-way feedback. Not only can the coach give the employee feedback on how they are doing but the employee can provide feedback on leadership and the leader's direction of the organization.

The key is for the coach to hear the feedback and act upon it. Feedback will cease if it is not received, processed, and dealt with in some way. Employees will feel disengaged from the organization.

Accountability

It is critical that the coach holds the employee accountable for delivery of their goals.

A coach needs to make it clear to the employee that coaching requires action and accountability on the part of the employee. The employee is accountable for developing and implementing plans that will enhance their development.

Likewise, if the coach makes a commitment to the employee, they are accountable to deliver on that commitment.

Support

Coaches need to be able to support employees in the achievement of their goals. For example, an employee may tell the coach that they wish to determine the best way for employees to understand the customer experience so they are empowered to improve it. The employee suggests an initial engagement at a retail store to observe the customer experience and an engagement in the call center to listen to the customer experience.

As a coach, you may think this is a great idea but you also need to make it happen. The employee needs to be given the time and resources to carry out their plan. If coaches don't give the employee the means to deliver on an agreed plan, they will soon lose their trust and respect.

Game score

Flattening the hierarchy, giving employees autonomy, and allowing them to self-manage, does not translate to leaving them to flounder.

Coaching develops connections and brings everyone on a collective journey.

Coaching is a critical competency for a winning soccer team.

Coaching ensures a meaningful relationship between the manager, coach, and players that is built on genuine trust. Decisions are co-created through coaching sessions.

Coaching will ensure that everyone understands the need to be adaptable and resilient in the face of constant change. Coaching checks in on the health and fitness of the players, and ensures they have whatever they need to be game fit.

PART 4

SURRENDER CONTROL

CHAPTER 25

Let go

In the following sections, I discuss how leaders need to get out of the way, and let go of the control.

Winning soccer teams would not be in a winning position if their managers and coaches didn't get out of the way and let the players get on with playing the game. If the managers and coaches maintained total control and directed the players not to take risks on the field, the game would be over. The managers and coaches give the players autonomy.

Organizations can only be responsive when they flatten the structure, remove the bureaucracy that slows them down, and give employees autonomy. Decision-making is then distributed, and communication flows easily throughout the organization. Employee innovation, creativity and experimentation are embraced. Employees can self-manage. They decide what to work on, how, and when.

One of the biggest challenges facing organizations wishing to create this autonomous workplace is getting managers to let go. Managers need to become leaders and surrender control.

The *Let Go Model* below illustrates that respected leadership comes when managers surrender control and are prepared to tolerate risks.

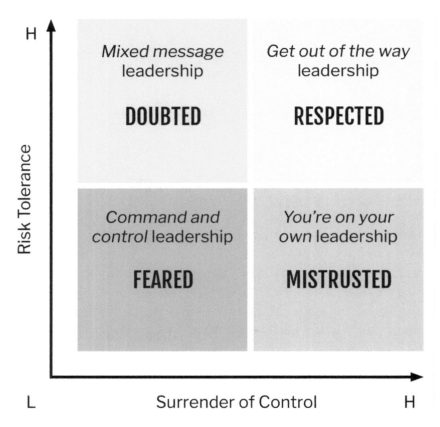

Leaders have to 'get out of the way' and give employees autonomy, delegate decision-making, and allow them to self-manage. Great leaders inspire, and then get out of the way.

There are two aspects to letting go, which moves a leader from one that is mistrusted, feared, or doubted, to one that is respected. These are:

* Surrender of control

* Risk tolerance

Surrender of control

If we are to become the responsive organization that we need to be, we require leaders who let go and surrender control. This is easier said than done. It starts with an understanding that when leaders surrender control they also release the potential in others.

When leaders surrender control, they delegate and establish trust. When leaders establish trust, they inspire and motivate. This leads to increased speed and ability to change direction quickly, rapid decision-making, and alignment of individual outcomes with organizational outcomes.

This is exactly what is needed to survive in a VUCA world. Leaders have to realize that their ability to influence will reap much more than their ability to control.

Control just slows everything down and leaders become bottlenecks. The organization is suffocated. Surrender brings speed, innovation, creativity, and collaboration. Control brings frustration, cynicism, disengagement, and mistrust.

Risk tolerance

Leaders need to get out of the way and let employees take calculated risks. Leaders like Jim Donald let employees take risks without adverse recourse.

When Jim became CEO of Extended Stay Hotels in 2012, he noted that employees where in fear of losing their jobs. The organization had emerged from bankruptcy in 2010 and so employees were aware of the financial pressures and the potential for redundancies.

Jim realized that this fear was restricting creative thinking and innovation. He wanted employees who dared to do something different and would take calculated gambles.

In order to foster this behavior, he had several thousand 'get out of jail free' cards (from the Monopoly game) printed, and he gave them to his 9000+ employees. The idea was that when an employee took a big risk on behalf of the business, they could call in the card and no questions would be asked.

These cards were a safety net to let people know that they could take a risk. One hotel manager in New Jersey did just this. She took the risk of cold calling a film production company who were rumored to be soon filming in her city. The company ended up booking $250,000 in accommodation at her hotel.

The employee knows best

Think of it for a minute. Who knows best about what is going on in the organization? There are countless times when the employee knows more about what is going on because they are closer to it.

Who is best to respond to a customer enquiry about the specifications of product ABC? The leader or the product support guy? Who is best suited to answer questions related to the agricultural productivity of farm ABC? The leader or the farmer?

Leaders need to get out of the way and let those best placed to get on with their jobs.

Game score

There are essentially two types of leadership. They are leadership by control and leadership by surrendering control.

When leaders surrender control, they increase their influence and effectiveness as a leader.

Surrender of control gives employees a sense of ownership of outcomes, a feeling of trust and mutual respect is established, and it allows ideas to germinate from a myriad of people and places. Creativity and innovation will abound.

Managers and coaches of winning teams let go. They surrender control once the players are on the pitch and allow them to play the game as they see fit and take risks as needed in order to win the game.

CHAPTER 26

Feared leader

When leaders retain control and are intolerant of risk, their management style is that of command and control. I should call them managers rather than leaders because managers manage tasks while leaders lead people. However, for now, I will call them 'leaders'.

Unfortunately, we continue to associate the title 'leader' with those who rule with a forceful command and control style. Look no further than Hitler as a perfect example of someone who led by fear. He was able to gain so much power by instilling such fear into his people that they had no choice but to comply.

The attraction of being a feared leader is observant, compliant, and obedient employees. This type of leadership might encourage employees to obey and follow the rules, but it will certainly not create a harmonious relationship between employee and leader.

Just as leadership through fear has no place in organizations today, it has no place on the soccer team. Teams do not win when managers try to maintain total control and are risk adverse. The winning team has to take risks. Some risk taking may pay off while some may not. When faced with a fast-paced changing and shifting environment, players have to grab a potential opportunity and run with it. If they don't, the competition will be all over them.

Feared leaders will not gain the trust of employees. Effective leadership requires trust and respect.

Command and control

Command and control leadership uses policies, process, and procedures accompanied by tight measures, to control the organization. Measures could include hours in the office, number of calls answered, number of calls made, budget etc. It is authoritative with a top-down approach, which sits well in bureaucratic organizations with a hierarchical structure. Power sits at the top.

Command and control stifles innovation, experimentation, and creativity, all of which are needed when organizations have to stay ahead of the game. Whether that be commercial organizations remaining competitive or government agencies needing to respond rapidly to the demands of its citizens, command and control has no place.

Motivators

Fear is not a good motivator.

Command and control uses extrinsic motivators including threats and authority. This will replace employees' intrinsic motivation. When employees have autonomy and ownership of their work, they are engaged, motivated, and productive. There is increased collaboration and teamwork.

Employees do not have respect for someone who assumes they know better than everyone. Employees know a lot more about their area of expertise than their senior management.

Challenges

Despite the myriad of books and articles that have been written about the need to move from a command and control management style to a more people centred leadership approach, command and control still pervades many organizations.

Many leaders know what they need to do but it is the fear of losing control that stops them from doing it. Leaders have to relinquish control to others and trust employees to do the right thing. However, when stress is the result of constant and unpredictable change, the natural tendency is to revert to behavior that feels safe and less risky; therefore, they are more controlling.

Mixed messages

The other issue with a command and control leadership approach is that employees will receive mixed messages.

Survival in a VUCA world requires distributed decision-making, self-management, innovation, creativity, and experimentation for the organization to respond rapidly to marketplace and environmental changes.

The problem is that by asking employees to act in this way while maintaining a command and control approach not only constrains employees but also sends mixed messages. The leader is asking the employee to do something they are not permitted to do.

Results

The result is disengaged and unmotivated employees. They will leave the organization. The organization will be unable to retain and attract the talent they need.

Productivity will fall while attrition increases.

What is needed?

Leadership is not just about having a position of authority. A true leader has to earn the trust and respect of employees. Leaders do this through delegating decision-making and giving employees the opportunity to implement their own ideas.

Leaders have to trust and let go. They need to earn the respect of their employees. There is no place for *my way or the highway* anymore.

Leaders may need help to move into this new world, so organizations need to make sure they get it. It's not an investment they can avoid.

Game score

Change is now constant and unpredictable. We need to create and innovate in order to not only survive but also thrive.

This will only happen when employees have autonomy, can self-manage and are encouraged to make-decisions, innovate, and experiment. Command and control leaders have to let go.

Feared leaders have no place in the workforce today. Nor do feared leaders have a place on the winning soccer team. Fear does not motivate anyone. Managers and coaches need to ensure the players can experiment and be innovative and creative if they are to stay ahead of the competition.

CHAPTER 27

Doubted leader

Mixed messages

When a leader 'says' they are risk tolerant and will encourage innovation, experimentation, and creativity but have low or no surrender of control, employees get mixed messages.

Employees are constrained due to a leader maintaining control over what they can and can't do. They have no freedom to make decisions as the leader retains the decision-making.

When people receive mixed messages, they are emotional, confused and conflicted. Conflict happens when we think a message is going one way (good) but turns out to be going another way (bad).

Common responses to mixed messages are frustration and anger. Other reactions can include withdrawal and shutting down until there is clarity of message, which might never occur.

Employees will doubt the leader's intention. Leaders often exacerbate the situation by pretending that the messages are consistent and do not permit any discussion about it to take place.

Soccer managers and coaches will not have a winning team if they send mixed messages to the players. They cannot tell the players that they encourage innovation and creativity on the field and then manage through a command and control approach. The message heard is 'be innovative but do it my way.' Any hope of innovation and creativity on the field will be killed. That team is only going in one direction, and that is down.

The doubted leader

The doubted leader will drive their employees mad by saying 'self-manage, be innovative, and take risks' while also saying 'plan and only deliver on the tasks I give you.' The doubted leader needs to *acknowledge* that this conflict exists. This conflict can be amplified in so many ways and can penetrate into external bodies including customers, consumers, potential employees, and stakeholders.

We all deal with mixed messages, all the time: Mum said one thing and Dad said another. But it becomes a problem when the perceived authority acts as if their messages are not in conflict and prevent any discussion of the matter.

The doubted leader needs to acknowledge that when employees appear frustrated, angry, or confused, it could be that they are receiving mixed messages. The doubted leader needs to *discuss* it. This doesn't mean that the mixed message will change because it most likely won't—at least in the short-term. The message doesn't have to change immediately. If it is being recognized and talked about, the frustration starts to be relieved.

The doubted leader can now change the message. They can let employees know they have received the changed message and they sense that it is unambiguous and consistent. They can take on board their feedback and act on it. They can regularly check in and ask if messages are clear and consistent. They can create an environment of openness in which employees feel they can call it out when mixed messages are received.

Not only will the doubted leader find out a tremendous amount about their communication style, they will also increase the level of trust between themselves and their employees.

When the doubted leader removes the frustration, confusion, and doubt, they should share this with their colleagues who may also be sending mixed messages to *their* teams. They should spread the word about their behavior modification and help change that of the organization.

Employee of the doubted leader

But what if you are a member of a team being led by a leader who is doubted due to their mixed messages?

If you are feeling the frustration, anger, and doubt. What can you do?

You need to acknowledge the situation. The problem isn't so much with the mixed message, but that you cannot confront it. So acknowledge the craziness of the situation. Share it and joke about it with affable colleagues. Free yourself from the psychological effects and don't let the mixed message mess with your head.

First, try and raise the issue in a light-hearted way. Joke about the fact that you need to do something but also not do it. Regardless of the outcome, the awareness has been raised and further discussion can take place. The issue has been placed on the table.

Employees need to work with the leader and demonstrate they really are trying to do the right thing. Employees need to remain positive and work through the situation. Employees can offer to assist the leader in removing the mixed messages. If nothing seems to work, then the only options may be to seek out the help of someone else in the organization, escalate the situation to where some action could be taken, or lastly, change your leader. The latter should be the option when all else has failed and you need to alleviate yourself of the increasing frustration and associated stress.

Game score

Leaders who send mixed messages (by encouraging risk taking while at the same time maintaining a high level of control) cause frustration, anger, and confusion. Employee engagement will be damaged and the organization will not innovate. It will become dormant and die.

Doubted leaders have no place in the workforce today.

Managers and coaches cannot afford to send players mixed messages. If players think they are being encouraged to innovate and take a chance to win the game but the manager and coach are dictating to them how to play, there will be uncertainty and frustration. This is a team doomed to lose.

CHAPTER 28

Mistrusted leader

Mixed messages

The mistrusted leader does the opposite to the doubted leader. When a leader 'says' their employees can self-manage, make decisions, innovate, experiment, and create but also that risk will not be tolerated, they are sending mixed messages.

When a leader 'says' their employees are autonomous but risk will not be tolerated, they are sending inconsistent messages.

The manager or coach of a soccer team cannot afford to send inconsistent messages to the players if they want the team to win. They cannot tell the players that they can make decisions during the game and then chastise them if it didn't play out as planned.

The mistrusted leader is saying *I give you freedom but I will not tolerate risk*. This is 'you are on your own' leadership.

Carrots

Mistrusted leaders are dangling carrots. They are promising their employees self-management and autonomy to do the job the way they want, where they want, and when they want. These things motivate employees. But by not tolerating risk, leaders are failing to deliver on those promises.

When employees are given autonomy and are encouraged to innovate and experiment, they are also being encouraged to take risks. If an innovation or experiment fails, that is ok, as long as the interests of the organization and its employees are forefront of mind.

When promises are not delivered, the trust of the employee is violated.

Money can't buy you ~~love~~ trust

Leaders can't buy the trust of employees by making false promises. With the pace of change in organizations today, trust is inherently important. Trust has to be earned. Leaders need to develop a tolerance of risk and recognize good and well-intended work regardless of the outcome.

Leaders have to provide consistent and clear communication and align employee work with organizational goals.

If leaders can't deliver on a promise, they need to be honest, transparent, and explain why.

Leaders lead rather than manage. They build teams. They use the term 'we' more than 'I'. They use the term 'us' more than 'you.' They constantly recognize achievements and provide coaching and mentoring where improvement in performance is needed.

Neuroscience shows that recognition has the largest impact on trust when it is given immediately after a goal has been met, and when it is tangible, unexpected, personal, and public.

Leaders need to be clear that they have the team's interest and that of the wider organization in mind and not their own interests and needs. Leaders have to demonstrate that this is the case. They have meaningful conversations with employees; they ask 'how are you?' and listen to what is being said.

When leaders don't know what to do, they must say they don't know what to do. They must ask for suggestions and problem solving ideas. They gives people discretion in how they do their work and demonstrates that they are trusted. Trust is a two-way street. If employees know their leader truly trusts them, they will give it back. Trusting employees to do the right thing but in their own way, is a big motivator.

Leaders need to be fair and show others that they trust and respect them.

Bottom line

Trust inside an organization builds trust outside an organization.

If employees don't trust their leaders, they will be verbal about it. They will leave the organization and tell people why. Customers and consumers soon become aware of an organization built on mistrusted leaders.

When trust is high, everyone is less stressed and people are more energetic and productive. They are healthier and there is reduced absenteeism. Engagement and motivation are increased. All of these aspects have a monetary implication.

Game score

Leaders who send mixed messages create frustration, anger and confusion.

Employee engagement will be damaged and the organization will not innovate.

Mistrusted leaders have no place in the workforce today.

Players receiving mixed messages will lose trust in the manager or coach.

When players are told to innovate and experiment but also that there will be no tolerance if they take risks, there is nowhere for them to go except to another team.

Teams have to be allowed to make mistakes and learn from them.

CHAPTER 29

Respected leader

A true leader gets out of the way and lets their people get on with their jobs.

A leader who surrenders control and has a high tolerance for risk is respected by their team(s).

The respected leader provides staff with autonomy—the right to work how they like, where they like, and when they like. Everyone is allowed to self-manage and make decisions without recourse to someone else. Everyone is encouraged to innovate, experiment, and take risks. In a world that requires organizations to respond rapidly to constant change, this is the only workforce that enables the organization to not only survive, but also thrive.

These leaders understand what letting go really means; they think about autonomy, delegation, influence, and innovation. They know that what they do or don't do, defines them.

Great soccer managers and coaches all demonstrate surrender of control and a tolerance for risk. They do their jobs, get out of the way and let the players dictate the play. If things don't go to plan, there is no chastising or blame. It is a lesson to the team. Winning teams have to innovate, create, and experiment. These things do not sit alongside risk aversion.

In order to gain control, leaders must relinquish control and trust their people. There is no greater way to lose control than to try to control everything. When leaders get out of the way, processes are faster, leaders are no longer the bottleneck, and employees are clear about what they can decide.

These leaders gain respect because of their self-confidence, clarity, availability, and their trust in people.

Leading examples

The following are examples of respected leaders who have earned that respect by allowing employees to take risks and giving them the freedom to do their job, their way. They got out of the way.

Warren Buffet, CEO of Berkshire Hathaway, leads 300,000 employees with a values-based, hands-off style that gives leaders wide leeway and incentivizes them like owners. As of August 2017, he was the second wealthiest person in the United States and fourth wealthiest in the world.

Then we have the already mentioned **Bill Gore**. The Gore website describes the leadership that allows everyone to create and take risks.

'Gore is a different kind of workplace. Instead of the traditional ideas of bosses and employees, we have leaders, diverse teams that work together, and personal commitments that each Associate makes — and keeps — to help our enterprise grow.'

Bill Gore once said, *'The objective of the enterprise is to make money and have fun doing so. Because of our distinctive working environment that fuels our business and engages our*

Associates, we're still meeting that objective on a daily basis more than 55 years later. We work hard to foster an inclusive environment where every Associate can contribute creative ideas and take calculated risks to explore new opportunities.'[1]

Gabe Newell, CEO of Valve allows employees to choose the type of work they want to do and tolerates risk.

The Valve Employee Handbook describes how its leadership tolerates risk.[2]

'Nobody has ever been fired at Valve for making a mistake. It wouldn't make sense for us to operate that way. Providing the freedom to fail is an important trait of the company—we couldn't expect so much of individuals if we also penalized people for errors. Even expensive mistakes, or ones which result in a very public failure, are genuinely looked at as opportunities to learn. We can always repair the mistake or make up for it.'

Ricardo Semler, CEO of Semco Partners, spent 30 years working on distributing decision-making authority to everyone in the Brazilian conglomerate.

Semco has become one of the most radically different companies. It doesn't have a mission statement, a rulebook, or any written policies. It doesn't have an organization chart. Subordinates choose their managers. All information is made public.

Bottom line

When Jim Bush took over American Express service operations in 2005, he became responsible for many thousands of call center staff members. The prevailing leadership style in the call centers was command and control. There were strict scripts to follow and calls were closely monitored. Call center staff was bound by the rules.

Despite customer satisfaction rates being tolerable, the competition was increasing and employee attrition was on the increase.

Jim Bush knew that every engagement with a caller was an opportunity to create an American Express loyal customer. When customers are satisfied with service, they will spread the word. This increases customer base, growth, and profitability.

So Bush got rid of the scripts and stopped the focus on call time. He decided the call center staff was best placed to determine how the customers wanted to be dealt with. Did they want a quick call or a longer conversation? It stopped being about call times and more about customer engagement.

He also started to recruit call center operatives with retail and hospitality experience rather then just call center experience. He looked for the right personalities and demeanors. The title of service representative changed to customer care professional, and employees in these roles had business cards, salary increases, and flexible working arrangements.

This success of this change was thanks to clarity of goals, guardrails or principles to guide the customer care professionals, fast customer feedback, and ongoing coaching and support for staff.

The return on investment included:

- Call handling time dropped
- NPS scores doubled
- Customer advocacy increased

- Employee attrition halved

- Consistent 10% annual improvement in service margins within three years.

In 2017, American Express earned the highest ranking in the J.D. Power award for customer satisfaction with US credit card companies for the ninth time since the award was introduced in 2007.

Game score

Leadership is not power. Leadership is not bestowed with the allocation of a title. True leaders influence and inspire. Respected leaders encourage innovation, experimentation, and risk taking. Respected leaders put their trust in their people. They promote self-management and autonomy.

When an organization has respected leaders, it will be buoyant on a sea of unrelenting change and uncertainty. It will thrive.

Managers and coaches build winning teams by letting the players play the game according to their skills, capabilities, and the context in which the find themselves.

Command and control has no place on a winning team. Risk adversity has no place on a winning team.

Great managers and coaches motivate and inspire the team, then get out of the way.

PART 5

PERMISSION

CHAPTER 30

Evolution

If organizations are going to remain relevant, they need to evolve from a time when change was episodic, sporadic or emergent and to a place where it is constant. This is shown in the *Evolution Model* below.

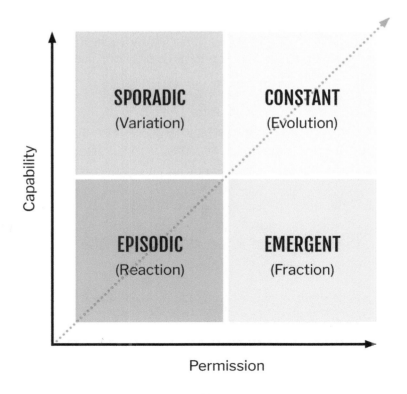

This is achieved through giving everyone in the organization the capability and permission to be self-organizing so that change is constant, evolving, and cumulative.

The soccer teams at the top of their game have players who are given both the capability and permission to drive change. Many would claim that players like Cristiano Ronaldo and Lionel Messi have not just improved soccer but have changed it. They have evolved in the face of constant change. The rate of evolution in their goal scoring abilities should have taken decades or centuries based on past player performance. Through capability and permission, they have changed people's expectations of what it means to be a great player.

Episodic change

When change is episodic, organizations are inertial and change is infrequent, discontinuous, intermittent, and intentional. Change is driven top down. It is often a new program of work or a change in strategic direction.

By the time this form of change is delivered, the information about the environment, competition, consumer, customer, and emerging technologies that informed the decision to change are no longer relevant. The world has moved on.

Episodic change is an occasional interruption or divergence from the equilibrium. It tends to be dramatic and driven by external events. Episodic change reflects the failure of the organization to adapt to a continually changing environment.

If the people within the organization have little capability and permission to initiate and drive change, where and when it is needed, change will continue to be reactive to external events.

Sporadic change

If people do not have the permission to initiate and drive change, the capability to do so is worthless. We can't have one without the other.

When change is sporadic, it takes on a scattergun approach and change is not targeted where it is needed.

We can equip everyone in the organization with the capability to identify, initiate, and drive change so that the organization can thrive in the face of constant change.

However, if everyone has to ask for permission, the rate of change will happen at irregular intervals in time and in isolated instances. Change will be non-continuous and infrequent.

Emergent change

Without the capability to identify and drive change, giving people permission to do so is pointless. Giving people permission to lead change but not enabling them to do so, will result in a frustrated and disengaged workforce.

Emergent change addresses the need to be responsive and adaptive. Change is constant but without the change capability it will be a faction of something bigger. It will be messy and inefficient.

Constant change

If an organization is to thrive in the face of constant change, it needs energy and ideas from the whole of the organization.

Everyone, at every level in the organization, must be in the business of leading and driving change.

The competitive advantage lies in the ability to constantly change in order to meet the demands of an ever-evolving market, competition, customer and consumer demands, and emerging technology. Everyone in the organization needs to be equipped with the capability and permission to identify, initiate, and drive change.

It is only through constant evolution that organizations will survive.

Constant change at Toyota

As of April 2017, Toyota was the fifth largest company in the world in terms of revenue.

Toyota has a culture of continuous change and improvement.

Everyone in the organization, from executives to shop floor workers and production line workers, are given the capability and permission to drive change. When they see an opportunity, they can respond.

In April 2017, Toyota's key financials in US millions were:

>Revenue: $254,694

>Profits: $16,899.3

>Assets: $437,575

They must be doing something right in a highly competitive and rapidly changing industry.

Game score

Just as organizations have had to come to the realization that change is constant and that they have to evolve to reflect the world in which they now live, soccer teams have had to do the same.

Soccer has had to evolve over the years to deal with changes in the environment, skills of the opposition, and the type of competition.

The rate of change has dramatically increased with advancing technologies, increased versatility of players, and the availability of instant information enabling fast decision-making.

In this situation, change is not led and managed by the manager and coach alone. Everyone in the team (manager, coach, and players) identifies the need for change, initiates the change, and drives it forward. The ideas and energy in the face of constant change come from the entire team.

CHAPTER 31

Permission to change

Capability

Most people inherently have the capability to identify, initiate, and drive change.

When working in their area of responsibility, they can see ways in which to improve operations and respond to opportunities presented.

We can provide the education, training, knowledge, tools, and resources needed to build the capability to lead and drive change across the organization. We can enable employees to self-manage, and we can educate them about the guidelines within which they can operate. The guidelines are the principles or guardrails that ensure employees are not hung out to dry when they are asked to drive change.

This capability often wilts and dies because it is not supported or nourished by 'permission'. The capability needs food and water (sustenance and nourishment) that allows it to grow.

The permission model

When we give employees the power of permission to change, we have a solid base across which we can drive constant change. Organizations that will thrive in the world of constant change are those that innovate, create, experiment, adapt, and have an agile mindset. In order to cultivate that sort of culture, we need a different kind of permission.

Permission must be heard as *'I trust you to do what you think is right. You don't have to ask me. Please go ahead.'*

The model below shows three elements that provide permission: empowerment, accountability, and delegation. These elements provide engagement, ownership and authority, which result in 'true' permission and a workforce that will be innovative, creative, and experimental; a workforce that will learn from mistakes and drive continual change when and where it is most needed.

The *Permission Model* below demonstrates how to foster an organization in which everyone leads and, therefore, builds a winning team.

Empowerment

I try to avoid the word 'empowerment' because I believe it is a buzzword often used but rarely truly affected. Empowerment should not be something bestowed upon a person as a reward for demonstrating initiative or doing something well. Empowerment should be intrinsic within the organization. Empowerment should be a fundamental principle and it should be core to the organization's existence.

Empowerment of employees requires a culture of mutual trust and respect.

There has to be a platform for organization-wide collaboration and communication. Knowledge has to be freely shared and readily available. Employees have to be given the skills and capability to act autonomously and be self-managing. They need principles or guardrails to define the boundaries within which they can safely operate.

Empowerment does not come about overnight. Empowerment is a fundamental change in mindset that has to be reinforced constantly with the right incentives and rewards.

Putting on the Ritz

The Ritz-Carlton is one of my favorite examples of true employee empowerment.

The third in a list of 12 service values for the Ritz-Carlton is about empowerment:

I am empowered to create unique, memorable, and personal experiences for our guests.[1]

The longest customer service call

Back in 2012, a *customer loyalty* team member at Zappos broke the company record for the longest customer service call ever. At Zappos, when you call for support, you don't get rushed off the phone because every customer loyalty team member is empowered to spend as much time as is needed to give the customer a great experience.

Zappos empowers every employee to connect with the customer. With 75% of sales coming from repeat customers, Zappos have a winning formula.

Accountability

Accountability exists when everyone (leaders and employees) deliver what they promise, on time and every time. They hold each other accountable.

When there are failures, mistakes are acknowledged and lessons are learnt. There is no blame or finger pointing. Accountability means that clear goals are agreed and employees are given control over how they meet those goals.

Transparency is required from leaders and employees to be able to talk openly and honestly about how things are tracking. There also needs to be mutual trust and respect.

There are benefits from employee accountability. These include:

* Improved performance
* More employee participation and collaboration
* Increased feelings of competency
* Increased employee commitment to the work

- More creativity and innovation

- Higher employee motivation, morale, and job satisfaction.

Accountability results in increased productivity and profitability.

Delegation

Delegation is easier to say than do. For many leaders, it is hard to delegate. There is a fear of losing control, a sense of something not being done as well as if they had done it themselves. There could be a lack of trust in the employees in order to delegate to them.

Delegation is a characteristic of a true leader not a manager.

Advantages of delegation include:

Better decision-making. When decision-making is delegated to those best placed to make the decision (those nearest to the action) the outcome is improved.

Faster decision-making. If decisions have to go up and down a chain of command for permission to act, there is a delay in the decision being made, which could result in lost opportunities or failure to resolve an issue in a timely manner.

Workload. One person cannot do everything. If a leader does not delegate, their workload will become excessive and they will not be able to focus on the aspects of their role.

Morale. Delegation shows trust and respect, which boosts morale and increases motivation.

Engagement. Increased morale, trust, and respect will result in increased employee engagement, which in turn reduces unwanted attrition.

True delegation is not only directed down in the organization but also up. Everyone should be able to assign decisions and tasks to those best suited to undertake them and achieve faster and improved results.

Engagement

Providing empowerment and accountability leads to increased employee engagement. According to a *2017 Gallup State of the Global Workplace* report, 85% of employees are not engaged or actively engaged at work.[2]

Gallup estimates that the consequence of this global epidemic is approximately $7 trillion in lost productivity. This points to the fact that the way in which employees are being managed and developed is failing. Most businesses today rely on the annual performance review to provide feedback on employee performance and discuss development needs and opportunities.

According to Gallup, *'The new workforce is looking for things like purpose, opportunities to develop, ongoing conversations, a coach rather than a boss, and a manager who leverages their strengths rather than obsessing over their weaknesses.'*

Empowerment and accountability provide purpose and development opportunities as well as focusing on employee strengths and capabilities.

Ownership

A sense of ownership results from empowerment and delegation. It is well known that Google allows its engineers to spend 20% of their working time on projects that interest them personally. They explore their own ideas and bring new products and services to the organization. Through empowerment and delegation, they take ownership for the outcomes.

There is a massive difference between an employee who 'owns' a piece of work and one who has been coerced into undertaking it. There will not be the same level of energy and enthusiasm about the work. This will result in a decrease in productivity and quality of outcomes.

Authority

Allowing delegation to take place and holding employees accountable provides authority. Employee authority can boost innovation and success within organizations.

Anadigics, a telecommunications component supplier, demonstrates the benefits of providing employees with authority. Back in the 1990s, the $250 million organization realized that its centralized, authoritarian control structure didn't allow it to respond to the increasing speed with which challenges and opportunities where being presented to them.

In 1998, the new CEO Bami Bastani distributed authority to employees on the basis of their capability to respond to market changes and make fast decisions.

Within two years of the distribution of authority, Anadigics' revenue had doubled and the organization reached sound profitability with quarterly gross margins improving more than 50%.

Game score

If organizations truly want to be innovative, creative, and remain relevant, employees need to be given permission to change.

Empowerment to change, accountability for outcomes, and delegation of work all result in engaged employees with a sense of ownership and the authority to make the critical decisions needed to produce quality products or services and provide customers with an exceptional experience.

This gives employees the permission to be the change they want to see.

To win the game, soccer players need to be given permission to change by holding them accountable, providing autonomy, and distributing decision-making. Without this, the only option is continual relegation until the team ceases to exist.

PART 6

GIVE IT UP

Chapter 32

Reduce control

Organizations today have to deal with the increasing speed of change and a demotivated and disengaged workforce.

When we have engaged employees who are able to utilize all of their skills and capabilities fully, we have increased innovation and creativity. When employees are micromanaged, there are poor results and low engagement.

Leadership with a fundamental mindset shift addresses this problem. Leaders need to reduce control and distribute power. They need to give it up. When leaders give it up, other leaders emerge organically based on their ability to utilize their skills and expertise. Decision-making is distributed to the place best suited to make the decision. This is based on knowledge, not a position in the organization.

Innovation, creativity, and experimentation are encouraged while mistakes are tolerated (if not celebrated) as learning opportunities.

Leading soccer teams are not in such a position because of consistency. They are there because they innovate, create, and experiment. They seize opportunities and collaborate on solving problems. They do so because the managers and coaches have delegated responsibility and they trust the players to do the right thing.

Many leaders fear they will lose control if they relinquish control to others. However, even if they accept that they need to give it up and start to relinquish control, there is a tendency to revert back to command and control in times of stress. So while initially allowing players to innovate, create, and self-manage the leaders then take back control. This sends mixed messages and a sense of lack of trust and respect. This leads to disengagement and attrition.

So in this VUCA world, how do we get leaders to move from a command and control position to one of delegation and trust? How do our leaders become effective coaches for our players?

Give it up Model

The *Give it up Model* shown opposite illustrates what needs to happen to move from a command and control position to one of delegation and trust. When we delegate and trust our players to do the right thing, we create an environment of collaboration, motivation, passion, creativity, a sense of purpose, knowledge based leadership, productivity, innovation, and engagement.

We move away from the command and control of manager to the delegation and trust of true leaders. Effective leaders are both a coach and a player and this requires a mindset shift.

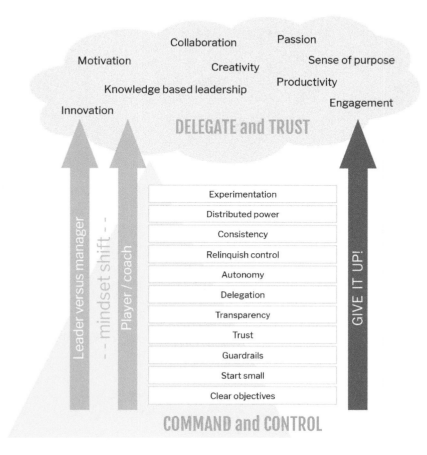

Delegation and trust: don't leave home without it

So what are the benefits of giving it up? When Jim Bush gave up the command and control approach in the customer service operation at American Express, he gave call center operatives autonomy and ability to make decisions based on customer needs. The results were increased profitability, employee engagement, and customer satisfaction, decreased attrition, and receipt of numerous customer service awards.

Bush achieved this transformation through elements included in the *Give it up* model. These included clear objectives, guardrails, transparency, and trust.

Leader versus manager

There has been much written about the difference between a leader and a manager. The main difference is that leaders do not necessarily have a position of 'given' authority. People follow a leader because they are inspirational and motivational, and because they build a relationship based on mutual trust and respect. People choose whether to follow a leader.

A manager is given a position of authority and people have a choice whether to follow them. People work for managers, they don't follow them.

In our analogy of manager, coach, and player, our managers are true leaders. For the comprehension of this narrative, I will call them leader-managers. While our leader-managers have to ensure day-to-day activities are happening as needed (management), they also lead.

Vision

The leader-manager creates a shared vision, and inspires and motivates people to turn that vision into a reality.

They are able to explain why the organization exists. Does it exist just to make product A, or does it exist to improve the life of others? What greater good does the organization strive to achieve? When this true sense of organizational purpose is elucidated, it can instill a sense of purpose into everyone.

Everyone starts moving in the same direction with the energy and vigor to make the vision a reality.

Risk tolerance

Respected leaders have a tolerance to risk. They are willing to try new things and allow others to do the same. Failure is accepted. It is a chance to learn and move on. The leader-manager encourages innovation, creativity, and experimentation. They accept that when mistakes happen, it is just one step on a journey to greater things.

Disruptors

While managers wish to retain the status quo, our leader-managers are ready to disrupt it. They challenge the status quo. They initiate, drive, and embrace change. They accept that constant change is the way it is if the organization is to thrive in the face of increasing disruption. They encourage everyone to look for better ways to work through being creative and innovative, and by embracing a mantra of continual improvement.

Hands off

The leader-manager doesn't direct people nor tell them what to do or how to do it. They believe in the capability and potential of their people and allow them to self-manage. If they need support and direction, they know they can get it whenever they need it but they are not micromanaged. They know that their people often have the best answers. The leader-manager recognizes that people nearer the action are best placed to make decisions and initiate change because they have far more knowledge about the situation than those in management positions.

Player/coach

Great leaders, like Steve Jobs, are both player and coach. A player-coach is someone who contributes as an individual but also coaches other employees.

Great player-coaches are able to balance their time between playing and coaching. They move up and down the player-coach continuum as needed. They know when to play and when to coach. It is whatever is best for the team.

The coach sits on the sideline during a game and has the responsibility of fielding the best team. The coach inspires and motivates, and develops the skills and capabilities of others while directing the game strategy.

The player is on the field executing the game strategy and utilizing their skills and capabilities, to their best advantage in order to win the game.

There are advantages of being able to move between the roles. Getting on to the field when needed can answer the coach's question, 'What is really going on here?'

They can get closer to the action while retaining the coaching perspective. They can be a participant and an observer at the same time.

Steve Jobs coached his employees. He would often spend time with the design teams giving them his opinion and guidance on their prototypes. He was also a player and his favorite part of the job was 'getting his hands dirty' on product design.

If Jobs had focused wholly on coaching and not playing, many of the innovations he gave us like smartphones, tablets, digital music etc. may have looked very different or not existed at all.

Clear objectives

Our leaders should set clear goals and objectives, and ensure that everyone understands what they will be held accountable for. Command and control management ensures that orders and work requirements are carried out by following strict plans and directions. We have to give this up.

Leadership is based on setting clear goals and objectives, delegating, providing autonomy and self-management, letting go of control, and trusting employees to do the right thing.

When employees know what has to be done and what is expected of them, it is much easier for them to work without constant supervision and interference. Employees make their own decisions about how to achieve the goals and objectives.

To the moon and back

A great story about setting a clear objective that guided and motivated people to deliver on that objective was that set by President John F. Kennedy when he delivered his now famous 'moon' speech in 1962.

In the speech delivered at Rice University in Houston, Kennedy said:

> *'We choose to go to the moon! We choose to go to the moon in this decade and do the other things, not because they are easy, but because they are hard, because that goal will serve to organize and measure the best of our*

energies and skills, because that challenge is one that we are willing to accept, one we are unwilling to postpone, and one which we intend to win, and the others, too.'[1]

He set a goal and clear objective, which many thought was impossible and caused considerable controversy at the time. Yet on July 20 1969, that goal was achieved when Neil Armstrong stepped onto the lunar surface.

SMART

SMART objectives will not be new to most of you. But it is worth a reminder to check your goals and objectives meet the SMART criteria.

SMART is an acronym for specific, measurable, assignable, realistic and time-related.

When President John F. Kennedy spoke before a joint session of United States Congress on May 25 1961, he said:

'First, I believe that this nation should commit itself to achieving the goal, before this decade is out, of landing a man on the moon and returning him safely to the earth.'

That statement has to be one of the best examples of a SMART objective.

It was:

Specific: *landing a man on the moon*
Measurable: *safely*
Assignable: *this nation*
Realistic: *nation should commit itself to achieving the goal*
Time-related: *before this decade is out*

Note that there have been many iterations of the SMART acronym since George T. Doran first wrote about them in the November 1981 issue of the *Management Review*. For example, 'assignable' is often changed to 'agreed', 'achievable' or 'ambitious'.

Kennedy's goal was definitely the latter as he went on to say:

> *'No single space project in this period will be more impressive to mankind, or more important for the long-range exploration of space; and none will be so difficult or expensive to accomplish.'*

Start small

When leaders are giving up the command and control approach, they don't have to give it all up at once. Giving up can be hard for many. Leaders shouldn't try to eat the elephant in one go. They should eat it in bite size pieces.

They should look for an initiative or project that is within their scope of control and decide to let go. They give up control, and set clear goals and objectives. They provide guiding principles or guardrails and step back. Leaders trust their employees to do the right thing knowing that if they need them, they can call on them. If that goes well, leaders can leverage the experience and do more of the same. If it didn't go too well, they can identify what went wrong and how to avoid the same mistakes next time. They use it as a learning experience and not one to beat themselves up about.

After each experience, they seek feedback from those people working on the initiative or project, and take on board what worked and what didn't.

Guardrails

In relation to giving up a command and control approach, guardrails are essential not only for the employee but also for the leader. The guardrails or principles allow the leader to let go without losing control. Instead of making the decisions for others, leaders create guardrails, which enable employees to make decisions for themselves. These guardrails empower decision-making often where the decision is best placed to be made.

The leader knows that the employee has guidance and parameters within which to navigate.

A flock of birds has one objective: to reach their breeding ground. That means they need to do three essential things: find food, stay on course, and stay alive. These are their guardrails. They don't have a manager bird telling them where to go and when. For the flock, they have guardrails, which guide them in regards to the actions to take.

Just like the flock of birds, employees have guardrails that provide them with autonomy to make decisions and a model that helps them stay on the road.

I have already talked about Google's nine core principles of innovation. These principles are the guardrails for all Google employees.

Amazon has a set of leadership principles by which all employees operate:

'Our Leadership Principles aren't inspirational wall hanging. These Principles work hard, just like we do. Amazonians use them every day, whether they're discussing ideas

for new projects, deciding on the best solution for a customer's problem or interviewing candidates.[2]

There are 14 Amazon leadership principles:

1. Customer obsession
2. Ownership
3. Invent and simplify
4. Are right, a lot
5. Learn and be curious
6. Hire and develop the best
7. Insist on the highest standards
8. Think big
9. Bias for action
10. Frugality
11. Earn trust
12. Dive deep
13. Have backbone, disagree, and commit
14. Deliver results.

These are 14 guardrails that keep everyone on the road and moving in the same direction.

Trust

If leaders want to give up command and control, they have to trust their employees to do the right thing. When this happens, employees feel they are an integral part of the team.

When employees have a leader who trusts them, they are more engaged and productive. Leaders need to trust their employees and let them get on with the job within the guardrails provided. Leaders must not then undermine this trust later by taking back control. Leaders need to be consistent.

Leaders have to demonstrate trust. They have to be self-aware to recognize when their actions may demonstrate a lack of trust. Trusting an employee doesn't mean that they know you trust them. Trust can be demonstrated by not admonishing an employee when something does not go as planned. Trust means tolerating mistakes and using them as opportunities to learn.

Leaders also need to demonstrate trust by not sending mixed messages. If leaders want employees to be creative and innovative, they have to trust them to do so within the guardrails provided. If leaders are risk adverse and not willing to experiment and learn from mistakes, there are mixed messages being sent. Leaders cannot be risk adverse and expect experimentation and innovation to occur. The mixed message infers a lack of trust. Employees hear 'You are telling me to do one thing but not trusting me to do it.'

Transparency

In order to give up the command and control, and move towards delegation and trust, leaders need to be transparent. Leaders need to share information. They need to be open and honest. Doing so tells employees that they are trusted with the truth. People often intuitively know when information is being kept from them, which translates to *you don't trust me.*

With transparency comes trust and respect.

Being honest is perhaps one of the most difficult ideas for many leaders. When leaders learn to be transparent i.e. tell the truth, they have to trust their employees with the truth. For many, this can be a very big leap of faith. If leaders are truly transparent, they are telling employees that they trust them with the truth even in the most difficult circumstances.

Transparency also means leaders share their own mistakes and challenges with employees. Transparency equals integrity, honesty, vulnerability, humility, and trust.

Delegation

To give up control means to delegate. When leaders delegate work to employees, they get increased productivity, quality, engagement, and motivation.

Delegation is more than just assigning a task to someone. Delegation is giving someone the responsibility for the outcomes you are looking for and the autonomy to achieve those outcomes in the way they see best.

There are some key rules around effective delegation.

1. Clarity: be absolutely clear of the outcomes you are looking for. Be clear about timeframe, budget, and frequency of communication such as progress updates.

2. Hear it back: ask your employees to confirm their understanding of what is required to ensure there is common understanding. This is critical for successful delegation and if not carried out can result in disaster for all parties. The employee might think they are 100% clear about what you require and work relentlessly to achieve the outcome, only to find out that what they are working on is not what

you wanted at all. It is devastating for both you and your employee and has an adverse impact on morale.

3. Ensure capability: ensure that your employee has the required skills and capability to undertake the job at hand. Don't make assumptions. There may be some level of training or guidance needed.

4. Open channels: ensure there are open channels for you to obtain updates on progress and for your employee to ask for confirmation or guidance. Be careful not to repeatedly ask for updates. Delegation means you trust your employee to get on with the job and provide you with updates as per the agreed communication frequency.

5. Coach: just like the soccer coach on the sidelines provides positive feedback and reinforcement for the players, leaders need to do the same.

6. Lessons learnt: the leader and employee should conduct a 'lessons learnt' session. What did the leader learn? What did the employee learn? What actions are we going to take to improve next time?

7. Feedback: leaders and employees should give each other feedback. How can each do a better job?

Autonomy

Leaders can only truly give up control by giving people autonomy.

There is extensive research and study into the effects of employee autonomy showing increased well-being, levels of job satisfaction, engagement, motivation, and productivity. This leads to reduced attrition and retention of talent within the organization.

Employee autonomy can vary from organization to organization. For some it means being free to set their own work schedules. For others, it means employees get to decide how they undertake their work. There are even organizations where it means employees can choose what they work on, with whom they work, when they work, and how they work.

Whatever the level of autonomy within the workforce, it should be about allowing employees to shape the way in which they work in order to perform at their best.

The focus is on what is done rather than how it is done.

The leader checklist for employee autonomy includes some of the things we have already discussed in this chapter. That is because none of the items on the ladder from command and control to delegate and trust operates in isolation.

The autonomy checklist includes:

- Building trust
- Celebrating mistakes and learning from them
- Provision of guardrails or principles
- Allowing for creativity, innovation, and experimentation—stop being risk adverse
- Giving employees ownership for the outcomes and determination of their own process
- Ensuring the necessary skills and capabilities are in place
- Platforms for collaboration—autonomy does not mean working in isolation
- Delegation of more work and decision-making
- Provision of frequent feedback

- Availability of open communication channels.

Relinquish control

Employees want clear direction from leadership but they also want freedom accompanied by loose guidelines and direction. Therefore, leaders need to relinquish control. Distribution of power throughout the organization and reliance on decision-making from those closest to the action is of extreme importance.

As I have mentioned earlier, many leaders find it hard to relinquish control because they fear they are giving up their power; they are risk adverse and they don't trust their employees to do the job as well as they would do it. The idea of relinquishing control is perceived as a threat. This is when we get the amygdala hijack. This was a term coined by Daniel Goleman in his book *Emotional Intelligence*.

We have two amygdala, one on each side of the brain. Their job is to detect fear and prepare the body for a response. The results include increased heart rate, sweaty palms, and shallow breathing.

However, in the throes of the hijack, we also lose perspective. Even if we can usually see different perspectives, we now only see black and white. 'I'm right, and you are wrong.' The amygdala prepares us for flight or fight and we, therefore, react before we can reason.

Leaders who can't relinquish control because they have been hijacked need support. They should seek out a coach who can help them on their journey. The coach can accompany them on the small steps that we looked at earlier.

When control is successfully relinquished, it can rewire the brain and reduce the fear.

Every small step forward needs to be acknowledged.

Leaders need opportunities and interventions that give them the chance to trial new behaviors in a safe environment. They should be allowed to take the 'risk' of doing something uncomfortably new and succeeding at it. Leaders need to seek out the necessary support for these opportunities.

When the new behaviors or actions are acknowledged and rewarded, the more comfortable the brain will feel about the new situation.

Consistency

Some leaders give up control only to rein it back in when a crisis occurs. Giving up control must be consistent. Instead of reining in control as soon as a crisis is perceived, the leader should create a renewed focus of utilizing the strengths of the people around them.

Gather the team together and determine how best to play the game and overcome the crisis.

Consistency is the key to good leadership. This means acting consistently, treating people consistently, and having consistent expectations. To do this, leaders will often need a high degree of self-awareness and self-management. When leaders are consistent, employees feel they will be fairly treated and this builds trust.

Inconsistency leads to mistrust, doubt, confusion, and disengagement.

Distributed power

Leadership Is not the right of a few but the responsibility of all.

Organizations that distribute power have new leadership practices that do not rely on the effectiveness of a few but the effectiveness of the formal and informal networks across the organization. Leadership can be spread across individuals and teams. Those not in a 'formal' leadership role can still be leaders.

Change can be driven from anywhere in the organization. This does not result in chaos as we have guiding principles or guardrails that ensure there is alignment, control, and risk mitigation. Everyone ensures that no one else makes a decision that hits the organization below the water line. These are the decisions that, if wrong, could be fatal.

The decisions made above the waterline may cause some damage but they can be dealt with, and they are not likely to sink the ship. There is room for risk-taking. The waterline can form one of the guardrails.

A great example of distributed power is from Bank Tabungan Pensiunan Nasional (BTPN). The medium-sized commercial bank was ranked in the top 50 of *Fortune* magazine's *The Fortune 2016 Change the World* list.[3] It also happens to be the only Asian Bank and Indonesian company in the top 50.

When BTPN set about defining its mission, vision, and values back in 2009, it did so with input from the entire workforce. BTPN leaders provide an environment in which others can lead. It cascades its 'customer first' values through the organization. It is embedded into daily business operations, its branches, and customer facing staff. This is achieved by actively engaging employees in problem solving, innovation, and experimentation, and allowing them to make decisions that ensure operations run efficiently and customers have a great experience.

Google has become the success it is due in part to the leadership style that communicates a vision and then gives employees the freedom to implement as they see best. It allows for boundless innovation.

Eric Schmidt, former CEO of Google made employees owners of their work by providing them with a broad definition of the organizational goal and then leaving them to it. He defined the goal as:

'Organizing the worlds information and making it universally accessible and useful.'

Every employee could relate to this goal. It was unlike a goal related to organizational performance like 'increase profitability by 50%'.

Experimentation

In a world of constant change, experimentation is critical. Innovation cannot exist without experimentation. Experimentation is at the core of the success of organizations such as Amazon, Starbucks, and Google. Some experiments work while others don't.

Amazon experimented with 'lockers'. These were locked storage units located in various stores where Amazon customers could collect their packages. Seemingly a good idea, some stores, such as RadioShack and Staples, rejected the lockers. So maybe that experiment didn't work as hoped.

Starbucks experimented with a high-end coffee machine called Clover for many years. They experimented with it in a small number of stores and when the experiment was a success, they bought the company that manufactures them.

Clover is part of the Starbucks internet-of-things strategy and has been rolled out across stores. Clover keeps track of which setting and coffee each customer prefers, so that when the customer pays by scanning their mobile device, the machine receives precise instructions on how to make the drink.

The Starbuck's internet-of-things strategy has included putting refrigerators on the internet so that employees are informed when to discard aging milk; wireless charging mats for customer mobile devices; and sensors in ceramic cups to understand customer drinking habits like sip size, drink speed, how much coffee they leave, and what they add to their coffee.

These all started out as experiments. Some fail and some work. But to stay ahead of the game we have to experiment.

There are clear benefits for fostering an environment for experimentation.

Better decision-making. When we experiment, we are basing decisions on real results, not just gut feel or theory.

A sense of wonder. The more experiments we conduct, the more likely there will be an unexpected result. We learn something that we didn't know.

Freedom. Instead of hierarchical control and inordinate approval processes, employees at all levels in the organization are given the freedom to have a go, and test out their ideas.

The challenge is ensuring that despite encouraging experimentation, the idea isn't stifled by leaders who revert to a command and control approach.

Leaders need to encourage divergent thinking—coming up with lots of ideas and answers to the same problem rather than stopping at one. They need to give employees ownership for the experiments and remove fear of failure. If employees fear failure, they will not be creative. Failures are learning experiences and should be celebrated as such.

Innovation

So now that we have climbed the ladder from command and control to delegate and trust, we can start to reap the benefits. Innovation is crucial to a business being able to bring new and improved products and services to the market and be profitable.

Markets are not just local, regional or national, they are now global and organizations are operating on a bigger stage with more competition than ever before.

Organizations that do not innovate could (if not will):

- Lose market share and profitability
- Experience decreased productivity and efficiency
- Suffer attrition of key staff
- Cease to exist.

The benefits of innovation include:

- Increased profitability
- Increased productivity
- Product and/or service diversification and differentiation

- Increase customer satisfaction and retention

- Market position and share

- Competitive advantage

- Attraction and retention of skilled staff.

Leaders need to convey the importance of innovation and its benefits to employees. They need to make employees aware that while innovation may appear risky, the fact is that not innovating and not trying something new is actually the biggest risk.

Leaders have to lead by example and provide employees with the time for innovation, creativity, and experimentation. They need collaboration space and recognition of their innovation efforts. There should be rewards for innovation even if the idea isn't implemented.

Amazon Prime is core to the Amazon business. In 2005, Amazon introduced the service that transformed online shopping. As of April 2018, the company boasts over 100 million subscribers. The Prime service was the result of employee innovation. It started when an Amazon engineer named Charlie Ward put the idea in a digital employee-suggestion box.

At the time, Amazon offered customers free shipping on purchases of a certain dollar amount or more, if they were willing to wait a few extra days for their order to arrive.

Charlie Ward thought some customers would be willing to spend more, and might even shop more often, if they could be part of a buying club that offered rapid shipping.

CEO, Jeff Bezos jumped on the idea and the rest is history.

Motivation

When we delegate and trust, employees come to work and say 'Game on!'

Motivation will happen when employees are allowed to solve their own problems, and create their own aspirations and expectations.

Motivation occurs when leaders:

- Give employees autonomy

- Are transparent

- Treat employees with respect

- Involve employees in decision-making

- Rescind command and control, and delegate and trust

- Provide frequent feedback

- Encourage and support experimentation, creativity, and innovation

- Treat employees as grown-ups.

So what are the benefits of having motivated employees? Well, employee motivation is intrinsically linked to high levels of employee engagement. Gallup produces a regular report called *State of the American Workplace*.[4] The 2017 report stated that 51% of employees in the US were not engaged and that employee engagement, as a whole, had only increased by 3% from 2012–2016.

It also revealed that disengaged employees cost organizations between $450 and $550 billion every year.

Motivated employees are committed and outperform unmotivated employees.

Motivation brings increased job satisfaction, which can attract and retain key talent.

Motivated employees will be more likely to seek out self-development opportunities to operate at a higher level.

Motivation improves productivity and efficiency. Productivity and efficiency are not based on employee skills and capability alone, it needs to be accompanied by motivation to do the job at hand.

Knowledge-based leadership

When leaders delegate and trust, leadership becomes based on knowledge. Trust overcomes the tendency for people to keep knowledge to themselves believing that it gives them a position of power in the organization and allows for the discovery and sharing of knowledge possessed by the whole of the organization.

Knowledge sharing gives the organization the competitive advantage. Knowledge-based leadership can take an outline of an idea and seek multiple ideas from multiple sources; thereby, using the full capabilities of the organization to solve problems or seize opportunities.

Knowledge-based leadership is about everyone in the organization having access to information. A lack of trust can increase risk when making decisions, as the knowledge needed to make informed decisions may not be available. Information must be equally available to everyone.

Knowledge-based leadership relies on open communication across the organization, the exchange of ideas and experiences, and regular dialogue where everyone has a voice and what they have to say is respected.

When organizations capture, store, and distribute knowledge, it stimulates continual innovation.

Resilience also depends on knowledge availability. When faced with relentless change, everyone needs the ability to act quickly and have the knowledge to make fast decisions. If decisions have to be referred elsewhere in the organization, opportunities can be missed and problems left unresolved. Therefore, not sharing knowledge is not an option. The risk is too high.

Collaboration

Giving up control fosters collaboration. It allows for collaborative innovation and experimentation. Information can be shared across collaborative networks in ways that wouldn't work in hierarchical command and control environments.

There are great examples of collaboration. We often think of Albert Einstein as a lone genius, when in fact the theory of relativity was a collaborative work of Einstein and his colleagues and friends. Two of the key collaborators were March Grossman (a mathematician) and Michelle Besso (an engineer).

Another great example is the five New Yorkers (two of them were roommates) who set about trying to not only improve the sleep experience through a better mattress but also improve the purchasing experience by being able to buy a mattress in a box— no more heavy lifting upstairs.

The five consisted of Parikh, the natural salesman (now COO), Krim, a mattress expert (now CEO), Sherwin, a brand specialist, Flateman, an online presence expert, and Chapin a stylist and expert in human-centered design. The five formed Casper, and in 2018, in only its third full year, the total revenue had grown to $600 million.[5]

It was the collaboration of the team and the diversity of knowledge and expertise that enabled them to solve the problem of how to create not only a great mattress but also one that could be delivered in a box.

Collaboration is a critical component of organizational success. Collaboration means that people don't try and resolve problems alone, they seek out the help of others. Collaboration results in increased energy and motivation.

The greatest advancements and the most effective decision-making comes about through the collaboration of many minds. In a world of constant and relentless change, staying ahead of the game can only be achieved through leveraging a more extensive network of knowledge, breaking down silos, and working collaboratively.

Creativity

Delegation and trust sparks creativity. Creativity is vital for business growth. Creativity combined with innovation allows organizations to resolve problems quickly and seize opportunities to stay ahead of the game.

Creativity can generate a sense of excitement and passion. It can increase curiosity, which increases a desire to learn. A learning organization is a leading one. Creativity is no longer a 'nice to have', it is a 'must have' for successful organizations.

Creativity leads to increased engagement, morale, collaboration, teamwork, motivation, and productivity.

Pixar Animation Studios' success is due to creativity. The company's keys to unleashing the creativity behind animated classics such as *Monsters, Inc.*, *Toy Story*, *Cars*, and *Finding Nemo* include mutual trust, honesty, learning from mistakes, and keeping an open mind to untested ideas so that new concepts are not dismissed before they've had a chance to be explored.

Passion

Passion is an outcome of delegation and trust. Passion in the workplace is important because passionate workers strive to do better. In our world of constant and relentless change, organizations need employees who are passionate because they have resilience and a desire to learn and improve. Organizations with passionate and resilient employees will have the resilience to thrive in our VUCA world.

Passion is the result of being allowed to experiment and to fail, having autonomy, giving up control, and distributing power.

Passion in the workplace is a positive and exciting energy. It is also contagious. When an employee is passionate and radiates excitement, others will look for the same. It can be a strong motivator.

Passion increases productivity, leads to creativity and innovation, increases energy, motivation, morale, and engagement.

Sense of purpose

When employees have distributed power, autonomy, clear objectives, and trust, they also have a sense of purpose. Whereas employee engagement was once driven by salary and working conditions, this has now been replaced with a desire to work with a sense of purpose. When employees have a sense of purpose, they are more engaged, committed, and motivated to make a difference.

Millennials entering the workplace are looking for a sense of purpose as opposed to a large pay packet. They want a meaningful job and the ability to make a difference through innovation. Organizations wanting to attract young talent have to create a sense of purpose through delegation and trust.

Productivity

Increased productivity is a direct result of delegation and trust. Employees not trusted by their manager will be less productive and more likely to leave the organization. Employees who feel trusted are higher performers and go the extra mile to get things done.

When the competition is doing more with less, productivity is critical. Leaders have to give up command and control if they want to increase productivity.

If we impose a process and dictate in a command and control manner, how do those people on whom the process has been imposed, feel about it? Do they own it? Will they try and improve it? Or will they just follow the process in a robotic manner?

If, however, we ask the employees to work out how they can increase productivity and give them some skin in the game, productivity will increase well beyond that achieved through command and control. Employees will own the process, be proud of the process and outcomes, and be continually thinking about how they can improve it further.

Engagement

Micromanaging employees will not result in engagement. Rather the opposite will occur. Disengagement is costly. Employees who are trusted and allowed to self-manage will be engaged. Employees need autonomy and support.

Talent globalization means that organizations need engaged employees if they are to attract and retain the talent they need in the face of disruption.

In our personal lives, we have autonomy to use technology as we like, talk to whom we want, access information in the way we want, transact when we want, and the freedom to live how we want. Then in the workplace, we are confined to use only the technology supplied in the way prescribed and talk to people only when they want us to talk to them. We are unable to effectively communicate and collaborate, and, in essence, are suffocated in a command and control hierarchy.

This dichotomy results in employee disengagement. Employees need delegation and trust.

Engagement increases productivity and profitability. It decreases absenteeism and turnover. Losing the best talent can significantly impact productivity and has the financial ramifications of replacing them.

Employee disengagement is not a choice, it is an imperative.

Game score

When we delegate and trust rather than command and control, the benefits are immense. Give it up.

Employees lead through shared knowledge, passion, and a sense of purpose.

It is the nature of the soccer game that when the game is being played, the manager and coach really have little choice but to delegate and trust if the game is to be won.

They cannot command and control from the sideline. The influence of the manager and coach is actually relatively limited during the game. If the manager or coach tries to interfere with play through physical contact with players or officials, they are likely to be subject to a touchline or even a stadium ban.

Winning soccer teams are built on a culture of trust and delegation. Without it, the managers, coaches and players should just pick up the ball, go home, and hang up the boots—for good.

PART 7

ADAPTIVE LEADERSHIP

CHAPTER 33

The adaptive leader

Not only do leaders need to give up control, they need to become adaptive leaders and be able to chart a course when they cannot predict the outcome of their choices?

Today, every organization is an information business. Leaders need to be able to read the right signals and act upon them.

Adaptive leadership is knowing what to do, when you don't know what to do. Adaptive leaders learn through experimentation and manage the context, not the instruction set. They cultivate a diversity of views to generate a wealth of options. They lead with trust and respect and provide autonomy.

Just as a soccer manager or coach understands that when change is constant, they have to be able to sense, respond, and act rapidly to stay ahead of the game, leaders in organizations have to do the same.

Soccer is constantly changing and evolving and the rate of evolution is increasing. Managers, coaches, and players may adopt the winning tactics of other teams or come up with opposing tactics to topple the opposition.

Only last year (2017), the English Premier League was responsible for the emergence of the 'back three' formation, the 3–4–3 (or, sometimes the 3–4–2–1), which plays with three dedicated defenders rather than the traditional four.[1] Chelsea manager Antonio Conte had always favored playing three defenders, but after his team was thumped 3–0 by Arsenal, he made the leap. Chelsea went on to win 13 consecutive league matches, during which time it only conceded four goals.

Other teams have adopted the formation including West Ham, Borussia Monchengladbach, Palermo, and Genoa. But each 3–4–3 is different to the other as managers and coaches adapt the formation to reflect the strengths and weakness of the players.

None of this, however, is new. Many managers, over the years, have experimented with the 3-4-3 formation illustrating how they continually adapt to changing conditions and increased competition. It was used in the late 1990s at Milan and at Liverpool in 2012 under Brendan Rodgers whose team struggled against the 4–2–3–1 formation of Basel. Following a 1–0 defeat, Rodgers responded with the 3–4–2–1 formation.

Leaders in organizations have to adapt continually to the changing conditions if they want to stay ahead of the game.

The *Adaptive Leadership Model* below illustrates what a leader has to undertake to become an adaptive leader.

A great example of adaptive leadership was when the crew of Apollo 13 radioed back to earth the words 'Houston, we have a problem.' They were halfway to the moon when trouble struck. That famous line led to a series of problem-solving efforts. These efforts were ones that NASA had not undertaken before. Because Apollo 13 could not land on the moon, the NASA ground crew had to process a series of 'what if?' scenarios.

The scenario they decided to go with was to use the moon's gravity to return the ship to earth. This decision was not a result of training, a handbook or standard operating procedures, it was the result of adaptation.

The NASA scientists had to work with the unknown and adapt to the situation.

Get off the dance floor

In a world of constant and relentless change, the days of making a plan and waiting for it to unfold are far gone. When change is constant, what seemed like a good plan yesterday may not seem like a good one tomorrow.

Adaptive leaders need to be able to change direction quickly based on a rapidly changing environment. Therefore, adaptive leaders need to be able to observe what is happening and make interventions when needed.

In adaptive leadership, this ability to perceive, observe, and intervene is often described as moving continually between a dance floor and a balcony. Ron Heifetz and Marty Linsky coined this metaphor in their book *The Practice of Adaptive Leadership*.

When on the dance floor the observation may be very different from when on the balcony. When you are dancing you are focused on the music, your partner and your impression is that everyone is having an awesome time. When you retreat to the balcony and observe the dance floor, you may observe that there are some people not dancing at all and there appears to be a departure of people from the dance floor when the music speeds up or gets louder. These are observations you could not make when on the dance floor. Now you have a clearer picture of what is really happening.

If leaders then want to intervene to change what is happening, they have to get back onto the dance floor and operate in the fray as opposed to above it. Therefore, adaptive leaders operate both on the balcony and on the dance floor. When on the balcony leaders take a step back and gain a clear view of what is really happening and can look at the bigger picture.

Adaptive leaders need to create a space where they can review and reflect on what is happening. Adaptive leaders continually move between the dance floor and the balcony. They are able to determine what amount of time to spend on the dance floor versus on the balcony. On the balcony, they gain perspective and make observations. On the dance floor, they make interventions.

Embrace failure

Adaptive leaders embrace failure. Adaptive leaders provide platforms that enable experimentation, learning, and opportunities to reflect on both success and failure. Adaptive leaders embrace failure as a learning opportunity and experimentation is rewarded even if the intended outcome is not achieved.

The key is to keep moving forward. There needs to be quick determination of why something failed and then move on.

Adaptive leaders and their teams become more resilient. They learn from mistakes and grow stronger. Success is achieved when leaders keep going and persevere through adversity. Failure is when they give up trying.

The adaptive leader's stance is if they are not making mistakes, they are not trying hard enough. Successful companies like Netflix, Amazon, and Coca-Cola embrace failure. We cannot learn unless we fail, and we cannot succeed without impediment.

Adaptive leaders give everyone permission to fail. It will energize an organization.

Leadership versus authority

Adaptive leadership is not about authority. It is about instilling a sense of responsibility for the organization across the entire workforce. Leadership is shared. In a world of constant and volatile change, leadership cannot be the responsibility of one person all of the time.

Leadership is everyone's business and is taken on by the person best positioned to make a decision or take action. Adaptive leadership is about allowing leadership to be distributed. Adaptive leaders develop employees who can anticipate what is going to happen, prepare for it, adapt to it, recover from any setbacks, and keep going in the face of adversity.

The adaptive leader has to model resilience everyday so that the ability to face relentless challenges, be positive and optimistic, and calmly react to stressful situations permeates throughout the organization.

Adaptive leaders create a shared sense of purpose and manage through influence not command and control.

Empathy and mutual trust

Adaptive leaders lead with empathy. They are able to see situations through the eyes of others. They are able to put themselves in another person's shoes. The challenge for the leader is not to think about how they would feel in someone else's shoes but how the other person feels in their own shoes.

Leaders continually need to ask 'Are you ok?' or 'Is everything ok?' Leaders need to be good listeners, impartial, and possess emotional intelligence. They allow another person to speak without constant interruption. They focus on what the person is saying and avoid distractions. They are impartial and non-judgmental; they put aside the fact they may believe what is being discussed is right or wrong.

They are emotionally intelligent. They are able to rise above the emotion in the conversation and put aside their feelings and the feelings of the other person to view the situation subjectively. The emotions in the conversation do not control the outcome.

Empathy is key in building trust. When employees know leaders will listen to them and take their thoughts and feelings into consideration, even if they don't initially agree with them, they will trust their leader.

When organizations have adaptive leaders, employees will share and openly contribute so the knowledge and experience of the entire workforce can be leveraged.

Empowerment: allow teams to execute

Adaptive leaders do not enforce rules and strict instructions on employees. When change is relentless and dynamic, we need a workforce that is empowered to make decisions and take action.

When employees have autonomy, they can react to situations intuitively and they will step up and lead. Therefore, the role of the adaptive leader is to create a shared sense of purpose, ensure consistent interpretation, and then get out of the way.

Adaptive leaders don't watch the clock to check the hours people are working. They recognize accomplishments not hours worked. It is about deliverables at work not duration at work.

Empowerment impacts the engagement of the team, which will also impact productivity.

Diversity

Adaptive leadership cultivates a diversity of perspectives. The leader considers divergent and diverse options and views ideas from employees before making important decisions. It is acknowledged that the knowledge of the whole is more powerful that the knowledge of the leader. This enables complex challenges to be addressed with multifaceted solutions.

The collaboration and involvement of employees in the development of the idea or option gives employees a sense of ownership and the knowledge that they are being recognized and valued for their contribution.

Some adaptive leaders encourage disagreement to ensure that assumptions are challenged.

Abraham Lincoln provides a great story about creating a diversity of perspective and encouraging or driving dissenting opinion. On the morning of May 18 1860, four men waited to find out who would be the next Republican candidate to become the president of the United States of America. Three, William Seward, Salmon Chase, and Edward Bates all thought that victory was theirs. Lincoln was not so confident. However, due to Lincoln's strategic positioning, he was elected.

The other three, who had spent their lives working towards becoming president, were extremely angry. Lincoln was considered to be from the wrong side of the tracks. However, when Lincoln had to select his cabinet. He included these three adversaries. He knew that in order to lead the country successfully, he would need their collective knowledge, experience, and strengths.

He used the diversity of opinions and perspectives in the cabinet in order to run the country effectively. When asked why he had included such strong adversaries in his cabinet, his response was simple.

'We needed the strongest men of the party in the Cabinet. We needed to hold our own people together. I had looked the party over and concluded that these were the very strongest men. Then I had no right to deprive the country of their services.'

In the same way, the adaptive leaders should not deprive the organization of the diversity of perspective within the organization.

Constructive conflict

As mentioned in the previous section, some adaptive leaders encourage disagreement to ensure that assumptions are challenged. They encourage constructive conflict.

Adaptive leaders do this to keep employees open to new ideas, opinions, and potential solutions. They encourage everyone to contribute and they build an environment of mutual trust and respect so that employees feel safe to participate actively.

The adaptive leader will make the sharing of differences the expectation, constructive conflict about issues, and ideas the norm. They will focus on the things people have in common as well as the differences they bring to the table.

Employees should be publicly recognized and rewarded when they are prepared to disagree with the direction of the team and question the thought process. This will encourage others to do the same.

Adaptive leaders often have to act as a thermometer. They turn up the heat when they want people to sit up and pay attention. They encourage constructive conflict but then know when to turn down the heat in order to reduce a counterproductive level of tension. They also have to act as a pacemaker. When looking to encourage constructive conflict, the leader needs to set the pace. They need to assess the situation and its context, calculate the risk of the conflict and then set the pace accordingly. This allows course changes to be made midstream.

The adaptive leader will ensure that employees are expected to present their ideas and opinions backed by supporting data and facts. The leader will provide a code of ethics by which conflict and debate are undertaken. For example, personal attacks on colleagues will not be tolerated, everyone's opinion is valued, and everyone has a voice.

Constructive conflict will result in increased participation in decision-making, better-informed decision-making through an increase in available information, increased collaboration and productivity, and increased understanding of others' beliefs and perspectives.

Focus

Adaptive leaders know when to change the pace. In a world of relentless change, there can be increasing pressure from more and more demands. The adaptive leader knows when they need to focus on the ones that really matter.

Adaptive leaders need to maintain focus on what is important and not get distracted by things of lesser importance. In a pressure situation with many demands, it is often easy to get distracted by the things that are easier or more comfortable to deal with.

When the going gets tough, employees can get distracted or avoid dealing with the challenges by passing the buck, blaming management, pointing the finger elsewhere, or putting their head in the sand. The adaptive leader needs to hold steady in the face of these distractions and refocus everyone's attention on the real challenge at hand. They need to keep employees focused on the priority work that needs to get done in the pressure cooker of constant change.

Timely response

Making good and timely responses is at the crux of adaptive leadership. In a rapidly changing environment, the adaptive leader and their employees need to be ahead of the game. They need the capability to detect, filter, and decode signals so that they can anticipate what is coming and respond accordingly.

Adaptive leaders need to make sure that the organization is constantly looking outside the organization and staying close to the customer, the competition, and the commotion of technological disruption. This is the only way organizations will stay ahead of the game.

The need for adaptive leaders to make timely responses can be likened to the military: quick decisions have to be made on the front-line. There is no time for deliberation. Leaders are combat ready and rapid decision-making is an inherent quality.

This is epitomized in Marine instruction. When you're 70% ready and have 70% consensus, act. Don't shoot from the hip, but also don't wait for perfection.

Note that the 70% is a metaphor not a strict metric. The message is about the necessity to balance deliberation and action in order to affect a rapid response.

The lesson is directly applicable to organizations. Adaptive leaders have to make quality and timely decision under complex and ambiguous conditions

The crux is that adaptive leaders need to intensify the agility of the organization to change direction quickly. This is achieved by decentralizing decision-making and placing it where it is best suited.

Employees need to be given the accountability to sense a situation, read the signals and respond accordingly. Timely responses will not occur when decisions have to trickle up and down an organizational hierarchy.

Expect plans to change

Adaptive leaders teach and coach their employee that change is constant and the plans we made yesterday may have to change tomorrow. Employees feel a sense of calm when plans change because it was expected.

When an organization is truly agile, change is anticipated, expected, and entrenched into the DNA of the organization. This agility is not something that gets added on when plans change; it is baked into the essence of the organization.

The ant and the dinosaur are both prehistoric species. The ant is still here while the dinosaur is extinct. The reason being that the ant was able to respond to a changing environment while the dinosaur could not. Given the large size of the dinosaur, the time to process information from head to tail, back again, and respond accordingly left them completely vulnerable to change.

In today's time of constant change and turbulence, agility and anticipation of change are crucial to survival. Organizations with inertia will end up like the dinosaurs.

Clearly articulate intent

Adaptive leaders, while avoiding command and control management or micromanagement of employees, must ensure that the strategic intent and objectives are clear.

The adaptive leader explains the 'what' not the 'how'. Everyone must be aligned with a common goal and then left to achieve that goal in their own way. The goals must be clear and unambiguous but also credible and forceful. This should inspire action.

Adaptive leaders then keep their eye on the game but do not run onto the pitch to direct and play the game.

Adaptive leadership provides direction using clearly articulated intent to enable actions to be taken in line with the intent. The purpose is to empower agile and adaptive leaders to achieve that intent. Intent is centralised and execution is distributed.

Embrace uncertainty

Adaptive leaders must embrace uncertainty and adopt new tactics if they play to win in the face of constant and relentless change.

Leaders must lead with uncertainty and be honest about it at the same time. If leaders cannot embrace uncertainty, and, instead they display overconfidence in a particular outcome, which may not arise, employees will lose trust in their leader. They will also disengage.

Using overconfidence as a protector means leaders are likely to make risky and costly decisions.

Adaptive leaders represent the truth and share this with their teams. When there is uncertainty, it is shared. This demonstrates authentic leadership. Teams that work for adaptive leaders who openly communicate uncertainty and seek team input to address the challenge are more engaged and loyal to the organization. Teams know that we are living in a turbulent world so they will immediately see through an overly confident, all knowing leader as false reality.

When change is uncertain, ambiguous, and constant, the successful adaptive leader will lead the team through the confusion and admit to not having all the answers. They will then call on the collective knowledge of the team to address the uncertainty. This demonstration of vulnerability establishes a sense of trust and mutual respect.

Game score

Leadership in the face of volatile, uncertain, complex, and ambiguous change has to be adaptive.

Adaptive leaders need to know when to operate in the fray, and when to get off the field and watch from the sideline.

This will embrace losing a game as a learning opportunity and the team will bounce back ready to play the next game. They will have empathy and be able to walk in another's shoes to understand their perspective. Players are inspired to be accountable and make decisions.

Adaptive leaders welcome ideas and solutions from the entire team and cultivate dissent to generate a multiplicity of thoughts.

Adaptive leaders know how to generate constructive conflict. They ensure that the focus on the tough and important challenges are maintained and that the eye does not go off the ball.

Like any good soccer coach, they make timely decisions in order to win the game and are quick to correct themselves. They give the players the decision-making rights to reduce the time between incitement and response. They get off the field.

Adaptive leaders expect and embrace change. It is their reality. The teams they build are dynamic and embrace change, and they channel any uncertainty into positive outcomes through collaboration and communication.

Adaptive leaders clearly articulate their intent and then let the players get on with the game. The players will ultimately win or lose the game.

PART 8

ADAPTIVE LEADERSHIP TEAMS

CHAPTER 34

Adaptive leadership teams

Leadership is a team effort. Everyone has to lead and be adaptive.

The concept of total football encapsulates the notion of adaptive leadership teams.

Total football

Total football is a tactical theory in soccer where any outfield player can take over the role of any other player in the team. It was made famous by the Netherlands national football team in 1974, when they reached the final of the FIFA World Cup.

However, Jack Reynolds, who managed Ajax three times between 1915 and 1947, laid its foundations and it has continued to be developed.

Total football could be described as 'organized chaos.' Any player can move into another's position. Another team member replaces a player who moves out of position. In this fluid and flexible system, no outfield player is fixed in a predetermined role.

Anyone can successively play as an attacker, a midfielder or a defender. The only player that stays in position is the goalkeeper.

The aim of total football is to confuse the opponent.

The traditional way to play soccer is simple: a goalkeeper, a line of four defenders, a line of four midfielders and a final line of two strikers. The ball is passed forward from line to line so eventually the strikers can kick the ball into the goal. Total football blew this system out of the water.

There are clear parallels between total football and adaptive leadership teams, which we will explore in this section.

The Adaptive Leadership Team's Model below illustrates what teams have to undertake to become adaptive teams.

Alignment

Adaptive leadership teams have total alignment. Just as a soccer team has a shared goal, the adaptive leadership team is completely aligned about the desired outcomes while respecting the diversity of experience, opinions, and perceptions within the team. They take time to become totally aligned and once that is achieved they have the same goal guiding their moves.

Every player is able to articulate that goal in a consistent manner.

Perceive and play

Information technology now allows adaptive leaders to read the signs (perceive) and react accordingly (play).

This organization has continuous learning embedded into its being. Adaptive leadership teams use experimentation and learning. They get continuous customer feedback to ensure they deliver what the customer wants and needs. Adaptive leadership teams are managed based on outcomes and a base of collaboration.

The soccer team has to perceive the state of the game, which includes pitch quality, weather, opposition fitness, and fatigue. It perceives the line-up at kick-off so that it has a sense of how it is going to play, perceives the strength and weakness of how it will play, and how that can be countered.

Adaptive leadership teams have 'scouts' who, before the next match, will watch the opposition and start to build collateral with all the intelligence gathered. The intelligence will be presented to the players and then the 'perceive and play' cycle continues. Intelligence includes speed and size of players, style of play, and strengths and weaknesses.

Information technology is also enhancing the ability to perceive and play. Numerous digital cameras now track every player on the pitch and collect 10 data points per second for the 22 players, which equates to 1.4 million data points per game. This data is analysed and enables managers, coaches, and players to gain insights of what exactly happened in each game, on and off the ball.

In the same way, organizations use real-time data to perceive what is happening outside the organization and what is changing in their industry. The data is obtained from data mining, market research, dashboards etc. and once analysed, adaptive leadership teams can look for indicators of threats or opportunities. Indicators mean they can choose to play or not.

Quality decisions quickly

Perceive and play enables adaptive leadership teams to make quality decisions quickly. They process the information they are presented with and can take action quickly, as needed. They are able to change direction rapidly.

Adaptive leadership teams know that in today's world of constant and complex change, there is no time for extensive thinking before making decisions. This does not mean they don't make quality decisions but they avoid unnecessary deliberation.

Adaptive leadership teams draw on the collective knowledge and experience, supported by available data, and make a decision.

The soccer team has to make quality decisions in the split of a second. If it doesn't the opposition will be all over it and winning the game will be in question. In total football, the aim is to confuse the opponent, which can only be done by perceive and play, and making quality decisions quickly.

Experimentation

Most organizations living in a VUCA world no longer have the luxury of a plan-do approach. It is now anticipate, advance, and alter.

Adaptive leadership teams experiment to discover what works and what doesn't. This facilitates the development of new products and services that move the organization forward. When they don't know what is around the corner, adaptive leadership teams avoid putting grand and detailed plans in place.

Instead, they experiment. Some experiments will fail and some will succeed. Failure to succeed will involve many course corrections along the way. That constant change in direction represents the organization's commitment to the development of better products and services through experimentation.

If soccer teams didn't experiment with different tactics and playing positions, the opposition would know exactly what their capability was and easily win the game by playing to an old and known entity. Without experimentation, it's game over.

Role fluidity

Role fluidity is at the heart of total football. Every player is prepared to move into another playing position as the game dictates. No player is in a predetermined role at any point.

Adaptive leadership teams move fluidly both horizontally and vertically across roles.

The players on adaptive leadership teams are able to play out of position at a moment's notice, no matter how long they have been on the team or been playing in a particular position.

Players understand the challenges of different roles; they have respect for other roles and empathy for their perspectives.

Role fluidity emphasizes teamwork and collaboration. It also raises consideration for flattening of the hierarchy and creating a more fluid, dynamic, and transitory grouping of employees forming around a particular problem or opportunity.

Role fluidity, the ability to move between various roles or activities, presents an employee with amazing opportunities and challenges. This experience not only enables the employee to grow and develop but benefits the organization from a more engaged, productive, and talented workforce.

Role fluidity can also reveal many other talents and skills an employee may have, which would not have been uncovered if they were tied to one job and title.

In our constantly changing world, static job titles embedded in a hierarchy will not allow the organization to respond. It will also cause employee disengagement and the loss of valued talent.

Shared leadership

'No more heroes anymore.' I am old enough to remember The Stranglers belting out that declaration back in 1977.

Leadership has to be shared and be allowed to emerge given a particular context. In a VUCA world, we cannot rely on a handful of people with grand titles to lead the organization at all times and in all situations. The leadership role can be adopted by anyone in the organization best suited to make a decision or take a particular action.

Again, here is Gore CEO Terri Kelly summing up the need for shared leadership:

> *'It's far better to rely upon a broad base of individuals and leaders who share a common set of values and feel personal ownership for the overall success of the organization. These responsible and empowered individuals will serve as much better watchdogs than any single, dominant leader or bureaucratic structure.'*

One measure of Gore's progressive, thinking-driven resilience is that in 50 years it has never made a loss and is consistently ranked as one the best places to work globally. Gore has no C-Suite, executives or managers. At Gore, leadership is shared.

Shared purpose

It is easier to win the game when we care about the game. If the soccer team does not have a shared purpose, it is not going to win the game, and all its players will play in different directions.

When we need employees to use their intuition and be autonomous in order to respond to a VUCA world, they need a strong sense of shared purpose.

Adaptive leaders are able to align the adaptive leadership team around a shared sense of purpose and value. Everyone then has the autonomy to take action.

Employees are drawn into a shared sense of purpose when there is a compelling and realistic purpose for the organization and an understanding of the ways in which the organization intends to achieve it. This purpose should be visited on a regular basis to ensure there is continued alignment.

The adaptive leadership team also needs to know how its actions contribute to the purpose. The team and the individuals within it want to know the part(s) they will play.

When there is a shared sense of purpose, work becomes more than just a job. Employees are motivated and engaged and will go the extra mile to fulfill the purpose.

There are a multitude of analogies related to geese and teams, and many of the sources are unknown. But the fact exists that as each goose flaps its wings, it creates an 'uplift' for the birds that follow. By flying in a 'V' formation, the whole flock adds 71% greater flying range than if each bird flew alone.

Teams that share a common sense or purpose can get where they are going quicker and easier because they are traveling on the thrust of one another.

Collaboration

Organizations now need a platform for collaboration. Employees already have the information, it just needs to be farmed and shared effectively.

Collaboration is also an eco-system in its own right. It extends across and outside the organization to suppliers, service providers, and collaborators.

When teams genuinely collaborate, they deliver change that matters. But a lack of collaboration and communication can result in organizational failure.

When change is constant, ambiguous and unclear, collaboration will be key to organizational success.

The environment and pace has changed for organizations just as it has for soccer teams and more collaboration is required. The soccer game has evolved and winning the game relies on more than one person. Gone are the days of Pele, Best, Beckenbauer, Donadoni, and Maradona who all had the time and space to take the ball up field and shoot at goal.

Soccer is a *team* effort now, more than it ever was before. Around ten years ago, European soccer players would be able to hold on to the ball for three seconds on average before passing it. Today, they keep the ball for less than one second on average before being challenged and having to pass it. If a striker loses the ball, they will immediately challenge the defender in order to regain possession. This has resulted in the space and time available for players becoming smaller, which means passing faster and interacting closer.

The only way to win is increased collaboration. Soccer teams collaborate on the fly and come up with novel ideas to win the game. Organizations have to do the same.

Game score

Just like soccer teams, organizations have to have adaptive leadership teams if they are to beat the opposition and win the competition.

They have to align around a common goal, perceive what is happening outside the organization and respond accordingly. Sound decisions need to be made quickly and teams will experiment to discover what works and what doesn't.

There is role fluidity and anyone can play in any position depending on what is required.

There is shared leadership with a shared purpose and widespread collaboration and innovation as a result.

When organizations have adaptive leaders and adaptive leadership teams, they are true champions.

PART 9

FASTER WINS
THE GAME

CHAPTER 35

The need for speed

The need for fast and iterative delivery of product or service is not going away anytime soon.

The big question for organizational change management practitioners, leaders of change, people managers, human resources professionals, project managers, and organizational design specialists is how do we manage the people side of change in such a volatile and often erratic environment?

Organizational change management practice has traditionally been designed around an episodic change cadence. This can no longer be the case and organizational change management has to move up a gear or two to keep pace.

Waterfall and agile

Organizational change has been wrapped around delivery of change in a waterfall manner.

The waterfall model is where each phase of a product's life cycle takes place in sequence, so progress flows steadily downwards through a number of phases like a waterfall.

The waterfall model was inherited by software developers from industries such as the building industry. Once specifications were agreed, steps would then include:

- Site preparation

- Foundation laying

- Framing

- Window and door installation

- Roofing

- Siding

- Electrics and plumbing

- Insulation

- Trim

- Painting

- Bathroom and kitchen

- Carpet and flooring

- Utility connections.

There is a sequence, and the cost of going back and making changes when a step has been completed is extremely costly or even impractical.

Also in the waterfall method, as generally in house building, all of the design work is done before any building (or in software development this would be coding) can take place.

Organizations that need to respond to constant change and change direction quickly depending on consumer demand, competition, and technological advancement have found the waterfall approach is too rigid and inflexible for this environment. Therefore, they have moved to a more agile approach where instead of a linear sequential approach, they have adopted an incremental and iterative one.

This approach allows for changing requirements over time. Work is continually prioritized to ensure the right things are being worked on to meet current needs and conditions. The value the business needs to be delivered is always being met.

Change is delivered quicker, more frequently and at a consistent pace. There are continuous feedback loops allowing improvements to be made in-flight. It is also highly transparent. Due to the volatile, uncertain, complex, and ambiguous world organizations now operate in, more are adopting an agile approach to respond to change.

When change is happening so fast, organizations need flexibility and adaptability consistently.

The dilemma

This is causing a dilemma for many organizational change practitioners and leaders who are grappling with the challenge of adopting their traditional approach to the management of the people side of change to an agile world.

Some of the biggest challenges I hear practitioners and leaders espouse are:

'How do we do organizational change management when we don't know what the outcome is going to look like and when it will be delivered?'

'How do we create a resistance management plan when we don't know who will be impacted by what and when?'

'How do we create a stakeholder engagement plan if the stakeholders are going to change as the project changes direction?'

'How do we create a communication plan when we don't know what to tell, who to tell, and when to tell?'

The answer is 'We don't', at least, not in the way we have in the past.

The traditional change leaders and practitioners have to become change managers and change coaches, and have a fundamental change in mindset. They must do the following:

1. Accept the ambiguity of the new world. Live with unknown unknowns. Embrace the uncertainty.

2. Be bold, brave, and buoyant. They will have to keep bouncing back.

3. Stop creating organizational change documents frozen in time. They need to be fluid like the changes being delivered.

4. Embed themselves in the agile way of working. Organizational change is not an add-on. It is woven throughout the agile journey.

5. Recognize the new type and frequency of stakeholder engagement required.

6. Move with the cadence of iterative delivery.

7. Give it up. The world has changed.

The *Need for Speed Model*

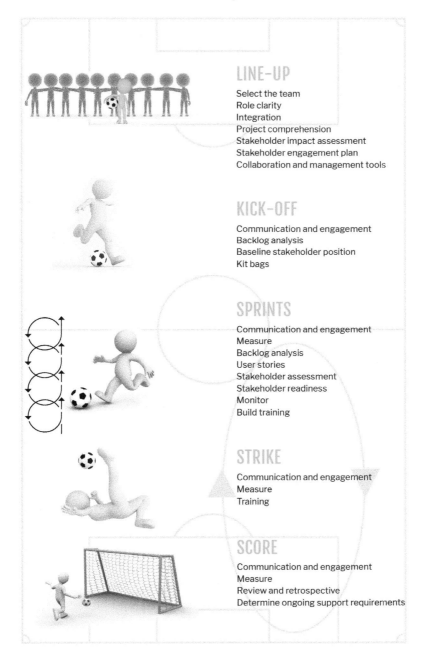

LINE-UP

Select the team
Role clarity
Integration
Project comprehension
Stakeholder impact assessment
Stakeholder engagement plan
Collaboration and management tools

KICK-OFF

Communication and engagement
Backlog analysis
Baseline stakeholder position
Kit bags

SPRINTS

Communication and engagement
Measure
Backlog analysis
User stories
Stakeholder assessment
Stakeholder readiness
Monitor
Build training

STRIKE

Communication and engagement
Measure
Training

SCORE

Communication and engagement
Measure
Review and retrospective
Determine ongoing support requirements

The *Need for speed Model* above depicts what the change managers need to enable and the change coaches need to be doing across agile delivery.

The rest of this book will focus on each of the activities to help embed organizational change into the agile world and effectively support the resilient workforce.

There are essentially five stages or phases within which organizational change management needs to be embedded.

- Line-up
- Kick-off
- Sprints
- Strike
- Score.

The key thing to remember is that organizational change management needs only to be fit-for-purpose. It will not be perfection.

Agile delivery contains feedback loops. One of the reasons for short and iterative delivery is to meet business priorities, which are constantly changing due to market dynamics. In order to respond to those changing priorities, agile delivery incorporates feedback loops. Everything the agile team does is monitored and subsequently tailored to address the feedback received. Feedback loops continuously review process, progress, people, products, performance, and the path to the desired outcome.

As a result, agile delivery can shift and change direction. Organizational change management has to be able to do the same. It has to be fluid, flexible, and adaptable. Therefore, when reading about the organizational change management activities taking place in each of the five stages of agile delivery, keep in mind that some activities may be skipped or undertaken in a different stage due to the changing demands of the project.

For example, coaches may not have time to construct all of the kit bags they would like to construct in the 'kick-off' stage. They may continue to construct kit bags as they move into the sprints.

Remember ... good is good enough.

Roles

The roles of managers, coaches, and players are used throughout the need for speed model.

The managers ensure that the model and associated tools are fit for purpose and they continually revise the strategy to ensure the players are resilient.

The coaches are integral participants throughout the model and provide feedback to the managers through continual feedback loops.

FASTER

Before we look at the organizational change management activities in each of the agile stages, I want to share with you my overarching guide for everything organizational change management does on an agile delivery. Change managers and coaches should live by this edict.

We have to change the way we do organizational change management. We don't have the luxury of weeks of preparation before something is delivered to the business. It is being shipped at an ever-increasing rate. We need real time, adaptable, and changeable approaches to change management.

It has to be FASTER.

This is the litmus test when managers and coaches are deciding on what approach or tools to use on an agile project. Faster is an acronym for fluid, accessible, simple, transparent, evocative, and relevant. When undertaking agile organizational change, managers and coaches want to check that what they are doing or producing meets the elements of the acronym.

Fluid

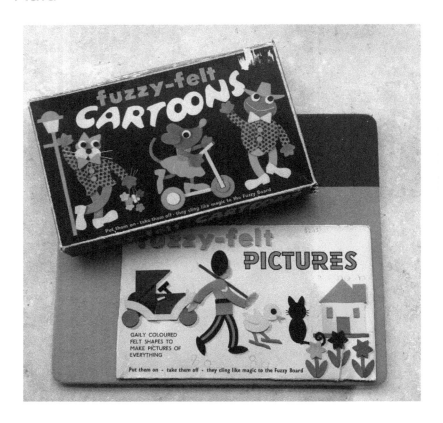

Source: Karen Ferris

Are you old enough to remember Fuzzy Felt? It might be a UK-centric analogy but bear with me. Fuzzy Felt was a children's toy introduced in 1950, which consisted of a flocked backing board onto which a number of different felt shapes could be placed to create different pictures.

As it says on the box, *Put them on – take them off – they cling like magic to the Fuzzy Board.*

Fuzzy Felt Pictures could be easily changed, dismantled, removed, and replaced.

Change plans need to be like Fuzzy Felt. They need to be fluid and easily changeable at the drop of a hat.

Change can happen at any time. Organizations have to adapt constantly to changing conditions, increased customer and consumer demands, increased competition, and changing technology. Therefore, the plans that accompany those changes have to be adaptable too. They have to be fluid and able to change to reflect new conditions.

Tools such as communication plans, that have been through multiple iterations prior to approval and have to go through the same level of approval if revisions are needed are not fluid. They are static. They need to be fluid—continually adaptable with minimal effort.

Accessible

Tools need to be accessible. Communication plans and resistance management plans that are hidden in the bowels of SharePoint are not readily or easily accessible.

They need to be easy to locate and navigate. They need to be intuitive. If they are not, they will become 'paper ware' and irrelevant.

They need to be visible. Whenever possible, coaches should put up tools and plans in high traffic, high visibility areas so they are accessible by everyone as they pass by. This will encourage conversation and feedback. It will ensure everyone is informed.

These are often called information radiators or big visible charts (BVC).

Depending on the geographical construct of the organization, coaches may have to use online tools to facilitate this.

Simple

Tools need to be simple. They need to be easy to understand. They need to be consumed and understood within minutes not hours. A plan on one page is far more powerful than a 50-page communication plan. A visual is far more powerful than a page full of words.

Which of these is easier to understand?

A **circle** is a simple closed **shape**. It is the set of all points in plane that are at a given distance from a given point, the centre; equivalently, it is the curved traced out by a point that moves so that its distance from a given point is constant.

OR

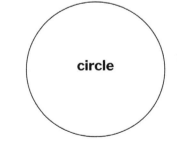

The brain processes images 60,000 times faster than it does text.

Rather than create a 35-page document, coaches will create a plan-on-a-page. It keeps everyone focused and aligned. It is a snapshot that can be absorbed in one take. If needed, coaches can augment it with a 2–3-page document that fleshes out the plan further. But remember, this will need to be maintained as it will also require changes when the 1-page-plan is changed.

When wondering whether to create a document or not, coaches should consider the value versus the maintenance overhead as that could crystallize the decision.

If managers and coaches want to get *everyone* on the same page, they need to get *everything* onto the same page.

Transparent

Whatever tools coaches use, they need to make sure that what they are showing is an honest picture of the situation. Transparency is key. Give people all the information, the facts, and the truth.

Transparency builds relationships. It encourages creativity and innovation.

If things aren't going too well and coaches are open about that, people will give feedback, and suggest ways to improve and get back on track. If things are going well, people will give feedback on how that can be built upon when moving forward. When there is transparency, problems are solved quicker and opportunities seized faster.

Employees cannot provide constructive feedback if they don't know what is really going on.

Evocative

Tools should be evocative. They should evoke a response. They should evoke emotion and promote conversation. Tools that evoke feedback can get other people to do the coaches job.

For example, let's assume there is a change that is impacting four regions across the organization. The change is undergoing rapid deployment to meet business needs, and increased consumer and customer demands.

Coaches want to measure various factors across each region but don't have time to do in-depth analysis, so they create a *Scorecard* based on their intuition. It uses a traffic light measure similar to the one shown here.

Measures	Region 1	Region 2	Region 3	Region 4
Awareness	●	●	●	●
Understanding	●	●	●	●
Training	●	●	●	●
Knowledge	●	●	●	●
Coaches	●	●	●	●
Leadership	●	●	●	●
Ability	●	●	●	●
Active collaboration	●	●	●	●

● Not started
● Uh-oh!
● Close
● Excellent

Their initial assessment of each region and the progress towards the behaviors or results they need in place to achieve the change objectives (Y axis) are captured.

The initial assessment is subjective and could be based on no more than gut feel.

If coaches place this in a high traffic area so that it gets high visibility, people will stop by and say:

> *'I just came off a conference call with region 3, and they are well aware of what we are doing. They are not red, they are green.'*

> *'The CFO was talking to the director of region 4 yesterday, and he was concerned that the coaching capability in that region was well under par. Perhaps they should be amber?'*

> *'Mary from marketing has just returned from a secondment to region 1, and she was impressed with the quality of leadership in that region. Maybe follow-up?'*

All that feedback enables the coaches to validate and adjust the scorecard accordingly. It can also generate conversations such as:

> *'That's my region. How do I change ability in region 1 to green?'*

This means coaches have engaged the person with the capability to make a difference and can guide them accordingly.

Relevant

Tools and plans must be relevant. They must convey something of importance in the achievement of desired outcomes. They should not just be displayed in order to fill empty space on a wall. As the old adage goes *If you have nothing nice to say then don't say anything at all.* They need to be current and convey something in which people are interested.

Tools and plans that lack substance will not solve problems or seize opportunities.

Relevance should be established by making it clear how the tools and plans are used in practice to drive decision-making and actions.

CHAPTER 36

Line-up

Organizational change management needs to get involved with the project as early as possible. Once the project starts moving, it will be doing so at a rapid pace, delivering minimal viable products in short periods.

Organizational change management does not want to be chasing a train that has left the station increasing in speed as it moves away

Managers ensure that the coaches understand agile delivery, and associated frameworks and approaches. Managers provide the support and guidance so that the coaches can be effective change agents within change initiatives.

Select the team

Well before engagement on any project, organizational change management should have a plethora of agile change coaches from which to assemble a winning team. The agile change coaches ensure that all the players on the team are change ready at any point in time and resilient in the face of constant change.

A change manager could be faced with three scenarios.

1. Established network of agile change coaches

   If there is an established network of agile change coaches, who have the skills and capabilities to be effective coaches, and a good understanding of agile, then the manager is in a good position.

   The manager can engage the coaches they believe they will need during the project. As the coaches understand the uncertainty of agile delivery, they will accept that they may not know what they have to do at a given point, or when they will have to do it. They will be on the bench but ready when the manager needs them.

2. Established network of change coaches

   If there is an established network of change coaches but they are not agile aware, then the managers have to undertake some education as soon as possible. This is why managers need to line-up the team as early as they can so they have time to bring them up to speed and get them game ready.

   Managers provide coaches with access to online training and provide a platform for collaboration, communication, and support. If coaches are unclear about something, they can ask questions and seek out support. Once this has been completed, managers will have a team of coaches from which to select.

3. No network of change coaches

   If managers don't have a network of change coaches, they will have to seek people who have the propensity to become effective agile change coaches.

276

Rather than spend time (they don't have) looking for such candidates, they should allow people to volunteer. Managers can put out a call for change coaches and provide a no-nonsense role description. The role description should be clear about what the role entails, and what is expected from those coming forward.

The attributes, skills, and capabilities managers are looking for include resilience, curiosity, communication, collaboration, flexibility, openness, transparency, self-management, embracing of uncertainty, open-mindedness, and the ability to effectively and confidently engage at all levels across the organization.

When managers get their volunteers, they will need to provide them with education including organizational change management, how people transition through change, and education about being agile.

Again, managers provide coaches with access to online training and a platform for collaboration, communication, and support.

Will the network of coaches be 100% perfect from day one? Probably not. Some will need more education and support. But if we have 70–80% good to go, that is probably enough.

A key mindset shift for organizational change managers is *good is good enough*. The 70% can help the other 30% reach the same level of effectiveness.

Train the team

Once managers have established the agile change-coaching network, it will grow organically. But the coaches need sustainment though continuing education, support, coaching, and mentoring.

Change coaches should be encouraged and given the skills to identify players that would make good change coaches and bring them into the team.

Role clarity

It is essential that there is clarity of roles well before a project starts. The product owner and scrum master (key roles in agile delivery) need to know what roles the managers and more so, the coaches, will play. There is no time to work out who is supposed to do what when the delivery is sprinting along.

While the organizational change managers and coaches can play many roles, it needs to be clear what those roles are. If there is no clarity, there will be conflict.

Some organizations have dedicated functions and resources for communication and training. While in others, delivery of communication and coordination of training is a role undertaken by organizational change management resources. Therefore, there needs to be clarity across the board in regards to accountability and responsibility.

When clarity of a role is understood, working relationships can be established. It has to be recognized that in agile delivery, sometimes the boundaries of pre-existing silos will become blurred. Not because someone is trying to trespass on someone else's turf, but because things just need to get done.

Therefore, it is critical to create an alliance or cooperation and collaboration with other areas involved in the agile delivery. These relationships need to be partnerships that are deepened over time.

Integration

Coaches need to be active participants in all of the agile (or scrum) 'ceremonies'.

These ceremonies are essentially meetings that take place at certain intervals in agile delivery.

CEREMONY	WHEN	WHY
Backlog grooming	Regular intervals	Prepares the backlog for the next sprint-planning meeting. This might include adding new stories, removing stories and estimating effort for existing stories.
Sprint planning	Start of a sprint	Product owner brings prioritized backlog, and it is discussed. The team estimates the effort involved and how much work can form the next sprint backlog.
Daily stand-ups	Once a day—usually early morning	Quickly informs everyone of what is going on across the team.
Iteration reviews	End of a sprint	Showcases the work of the team. Celebrates work done, demonstrates work finished, and obtains stakeholder feedback.
Retrospectives	End of a sprint	Used to find out what is working well, what is not working well, and how things can be improved.

Organizational change management needs to have a truly integrated and cohesive existence within the project and not be an add-on. Attendance and contribution by coaches at these ceremonies is an imperative.

Project comprehension

Coaches engaged on an agile delivery will need to learn as much as they can about the project while accepting that there will be unknown unknowns.

Again, this is a fundamental mindset shift for many. On waterfall projects, we know exactly what the requirements are, when they will be delivered, and to whom. While the project is underway, organizational change can develop comprehensive resistance management plans, stakeholder engagement plans, communication and training plans etc. This is a luxury that is no longer afforded.

We have to deliver as best we can, knowing what we know. We have to shift from a mindset of *more than enough* to one of *good enough*.

Coaches need to understand the project intent, goals, objectives, and estimated timelines. As best we can, we need to identify the stakeholders. We may only be able to identify 70–80% but that is good enough.

It should be remembered that on an agile project, the product owner is generally responsible for the management of key stakeholders. On an agile project, as the momentum needs to be maintained, key stakeholders are an intrinsic part of the project and available to make decisions in a timely manner.

Therefore, the key stakeholders are already identified. Stakeholders can include people or groups internal and external to the organization e.g. vendors, regulators, subcontractors etc.

Stakeholder impact assessment

Coaches need to do an initial, albeit high-level impact assessment for the stakeholders that they know about. Due to the transparent and visible nature of agile delivery, stakeholders can see what is going on. Key stakeholders will have been involved in the writing of user stories and grooming the backlog.

User stories are short, simple descriptions of a feature told from the perspective of the person who desires the new capability— usually a user or customer of the system. They are the agile way of gathering and building requirements.

The product owner, in conjunction with the team (including key stakeholders) performs backlog grooming. The backlog is reviewed to ensure it contains the right things, in the right priority order. The items at the top of the backlog will be the ones to be delivered in the upcoming sprints. It occurs on a regular basis.

Therefore, key stakeholders have visibility of delivery progress. Rather than just being recipients of a change, they have a real stake in it. They are actively engaged and involved.

The role of the coach is to deliver early and frequent engagement across as many identified impacted groups as possible. Key stakeholders can help identify impacted groups.

The change-coaching network can be leveraged and requested to indicate the scale of the impact on particular groups and identify others that will be impacted.

At this point, it might be as simple as indicating a small, medium, large, or extra large impact. The t-shirt sizing will suffice for now.

The first thing that should be assessed is the organization's understanding of agile. Do they understand the principles and practices? If not, organizational change management will need to drive the provision of education across the organization so that the benefits of an agile approach are understood.

In summary, coaches need to leverage key stakeholders, user stories and the change-coaching network to determine stakeholder impacts.

One tool that can be used to illustrate stakeholder impact is a blast radius.

Blast radius

Blast radius is a term used to describe the distance from the source that will be affected when an explosion occurs. A series of concentric circles indicate the level of impact. Fireball is at the center, air blast radius is next, and radiation radius follows.

In our organizational change management blast radius, we also have concentric circles to illustrate the impact of our change on our stakeholders. The detail on the blast radius can be added and changed over time.

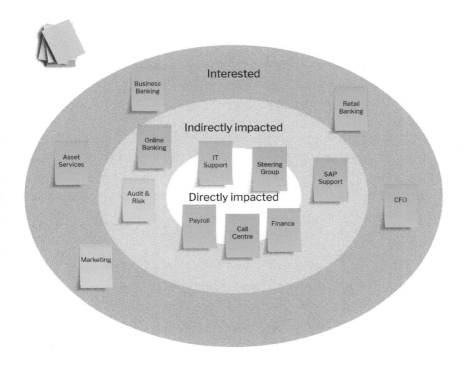

Blast Radius (inspired by Jason Little https://
leanchange.org/resources/blastradius/)

The above is a simple example of a *Blast Radius* for a change.

Sticky notes are used to place stakeholders or stakeholder groups into the directly impacted, indirectly impacted or interested circles. If coaches want to be more granular, they could use the color of the sticky note to capture information about the stakeholder or stakeholder group.

Coaches could use the colored sticky notes to denote:

BLUE for Blockers: The resistors are stubborn and tend to react negatively to change. They are not generally open to listening to arguments for change.

GREEN for Questioners: The questioners can be convinced of a need to change and will follow.

PINK for Promoters: The promoters are open to change and can lead change. They will be supportive of the change, and they can make great additional change coaches.

Of course, these are generalizations but if 70% correct, they can effectively guide the coaches' engagement activities and efforts. For instance, coaches would focus on the promoters first, as champions of change. This should be the largest effort because once they thoroughly understand the change, coaches can request them to engage with the questioners.

The questioners generally form 80% of the stakeholder group with 10% being promoters and 10% being blockers. The latter is the group on which coaches spend least time. Their mindset means coaches could spend an inordinate amount of time to bring them on board within a timeframe they desire. But this is time they don't have. They will adopt the new way of working, albeit reluctantly, because it will just become the way in which things are done around here.

Coaches may wish to add further granularity to the blast radius to indicate the 'type' of impact on the stakeholders/players.

In the *Blast Radius* opposite, four types of impact have been identified: people, process and procedure, technology, and culture. Coaches may wish to identify more, for example, policy, organizational structure etc. The guidance is to keep it simple.

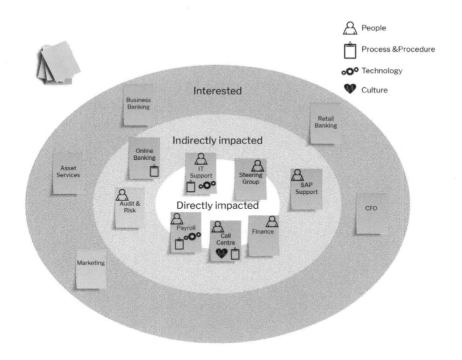

Blast Radius Incorporating Impact Type (inspired by Jason Little https://leanchange.org/resources/blastradius/)

The areas directly impacted and indirectly impacted have been labeled with the type of impact they will experience as a result of this sprint.

Stakeholder engagement plan

Influencer map

An influencer map is a tool that can inform the communication and engagement plan. It is a simple version of the power/ influence grid and can be changed sprint-by- sprint.

A coach can facilitate a workshop with colleagues to create the influencer map.

A large pyramid is drawn on a surface that can be retained for the duration of the project. A set of cardboard or paper circles of various sizes, marker pens, and drawing pins are needed. It is useful if the circles are of like size and the same color. The circles will be used to represent the size of the various stakeholder groups.

The coach then facilitates as follows:

Estimate stakeholder group size

Different sized stakeholder groups can be represented by different sized paper circles representing the number of people in the group (smallest=fewest, biggest=most).

Map stakeholder influence and relationships

This is the key step in the process. The circles are arranged within the pyramid to display influence and relationships.

Influence is shown by the relative closeness of circles to the pyramid apex, while relationships (degree of cooperation or conflict, and shared or divergent views) are indicated by the relative proximity and overlap of the circles. This step will take the most time.

The example *Influencer Map* shown below reflects the size and influence of stakeholder groups in relation to the introduction of agile project management into the organization. As can be seen, the largest stakeholder group is the 'rest of the business' but they have less influence on the outcome than the smaller groups of project managers and the project management office.

Therefore, the stakeholder engagement plan needs to reflect the needs of the high influencing groups.

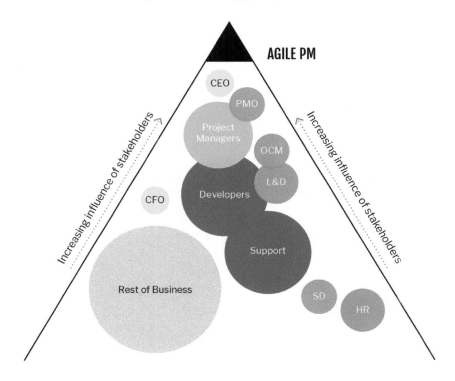

Engagement plan

Once the high-level impacts and high influencers are known, the coaches can formulate an initial stakeholder engagement plan.

Like all plans, it needs to be FASTER (see section 35). Think *plan-on-a-page*. The plan should contain the engagement activities that will take place with each stakeholder group and at what time. The change-coaching network will locally lead the engagement.

Remember that all plans are subject to constant change and revision. On the *Stakeholder Engagement Plan-on-a-page* below, the impacts, interest and influence, approach, method, and frequency could all change over time.

STAKEHOLDER ENGAGEMENT PLAN					
Stakeholder	Impact	Interest/ Influence	Approach	Method	Frequency
Marketing		Customer behavior change	Consult	Slack	End of each sprint
IT		New cloud technology	Consult	Webinar Slack	End of each sprint
HR		On boarding process	Consult	Webinar Slack	Weekly
Legal		Employee legislative requirements	Consult	Slack	Weekly
CX		Customer impacts	Consult	Slack	End of each sprint

Story-telling

Story telling is a tool that can be used as part of stakeholder engagement. Story telling is a great way to sell an idea or concept. Let's assume that as a result of the impact assessment the coaches have determined that the business does not understand the principles and concepts of agile delivery. Coaches have to convince them of the benefits so that they can embrace new ways of working.

Pixar, the Disney animation studio, has a tried-and-tested formula for great story telling.

Every story has a spine that goes like this:

Once upon a time, there was___.
Every day___.
One day___.
Because of that___.
Because of that___.
Until finally___.

I am not suggesting that coaches start a business story with the words *once upon a time* but they can use the formula to construct a business story in regards to agile adoption.

For example:

There was a time when the business started to fall behind the competition.

Every day, the competition encroached on previously solid markets.

One day, we realized that we could not innovate and deliver fast enough.

Because of that, we adopted an agile approach to delivery of products and services.

Because of that, we could meet customer, consumer, and business needs in a rapid and iterative manner.

Until finally, we obtained the position of market leader in our industry.

Collaboration and management tools

Managers and coaches should determine the collaboration tools that exist within the organization and leverage the most popular. Collaboration platforms include Yammer, Slack, Jive, Jira, SocialCast, Convo, and Chatter. There are many more.

Coaches should establish a community within the tool where information about the change can be disseminated in real time, and conversations and requests for more information or answers to questions generated.

It is important to remember that collaboration isn't just about technology. There are often areas within the organization where people gather in order to communicate and collaborate freely. These include dining areas, employee lounges, kitchens etc.

Coaches should also leverage these areas and use them to illustrate physically the changes that are coming. Pictures and metaphors work well in these situations.

Management tools will also need to be identified and put in place if they do not already exist.

Kanban board

The most common management tool used in agile delivery is the Kanban board. It is visual, simple and extremely powerful. Kanban is a visual work management tool.

Kanban is Japanese for 'visual signal' or 'card' and its origin dates back to the 1940s at Toyota. In its simplest form, it consists of three columns called 'To Do', 'Doing' and 'Done.'

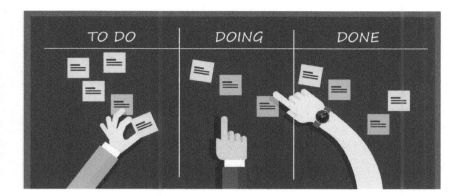

Kanban board

Cards or sticky notes are used to capture all the work that needs to be completed and are placed in 'To Do'. The work is then prioritized and delegated, and the cards or sticky notes can be moved into 'Doing'. On completion, the card or sticky note is moved into 'Done'. The process repeats itself.

Advantages of Kanban include the ability to limit the work in progress. The team only works on what is in 'Doing' and not more than they can deliver in a specified period of time e.g. a 2-week sprint. The visibility of Kanban amplifies communication and collaboration. Everyone can see what needs to be done and the progress that is being made.

Coaches may start with a Kanban board separate to that of the agile project team while they are getting used to the tool. However, I would strongly recommend that coaches look to integrate their activities into the agile project Kanban board as soon as possible. This gives one view of the project and organizational change management activities. The latter can be prioritized alongside the prioritization of project activities. This also promotes organizational change management as being an integral part of the project and not something that is added on.

Coaches may need online activity tracking tools that allow geographically dispersed or remotely located change coaches to collaborate. These tools could include platforms or applications such as Trello, Asana, Leankit or Taskworld. There are many more.

Whichever collaboration and management tools are selected, they need to be fit for purpose. It is important that managers proactively identify the collaboration and management tools to be used.

It is also important to have tools that allow coaches to track communication and engagement such as MailChimp or Campaign Monitor. These tools provide coaches with analytics so they can view the performance of their communication and engagement activities and gain insights into how to improve their approach.

Strategic change canvas

In this phase, coaches may commence creation of a strategic change canvas. We use the word canvas because the word 'plan' infers comprehensive documentation, approved and signed off by a number of people and cannot be changed without further approval. 'Plan' sounds static whereas a 'canvas' sounds more fluid and flexible, which is exactly what it is.

The idea of a canvas was popularized by Alex Osterwalder when he introduced the Business Model Canvas in his book *Business Model Generation*. The Business Model Canvas is a visual chart, and it removes the need for heavy weighted business cases, and is easily understood.

The strategic change canvas can contain whatever elements coaches decide they will need in order to answer the burning questions people will have when change occurs. The aim of the canvas is to get everyone on the same page.

NAME OF THE CHANGE

Goal

What is the goal? Answer the question 'What will this change do for us and our organization?'

Why

Why is it important to the organization? This is about creating a sense of urgency. If we do it then X will happen. If we don't do it, then Y will happen.

Success	Progress
Describe what success looks like and how it will be measured/demonstrated/felt.	Describe how progress towards the end goal will be tracked?

What will change	Support
Describe (at a high level) what elements will be changed, for example, process, people, tools, technology, systems, structures.	What will organizational change management provide to support people through this change? What will be the engagement approach, and where can people get support and more information. What will change managers and coaches do?

The plan

Is the plan based on what we know? This information can be extracted from the prioritized product backlog noting that it may and most likely will, change over time. Streams could include communication, engagement, education, training, etc.

Month 1	Month 2	Month 3	Month 4	Month 5	Month 6

Example Strategic Change Canvas (inspired by Jason Little http://leanchange.org/resources/canvases)

Remember, coaches will need to customize this to meet their specific needs and ensure it is fit for purpose.

Outputs

Some of the outputs from this stage may include:

- Stakeholder impact assessment
- Blast radius illustrating stakeholder impact
- Stakeholder engagement plan
- Kanban board containing organizational change management activities
- Strategic change canvas.

CHAPTER 37

Kick-off

Kick-off is when coaches start to communicate and engage. At this point, coaches may only be communicating intent, as until the product backlog grooming is complete and it is determined what will be in the initial sprints, it could be unclear about what is going to be delivered and to whom. What needs to be done at this stage is to create visibility for the change and for the change coaches to be actively visible.

The stakeholder position in relation to the change will need to be baselined so that coaches can determine the effectiveness of their communication and engagement activities going forward, and also check where the stakeholders are on their change journey.

Communication and engagement

This is where the coaches kick-off stakeholder engagement as per the high-level plan they have developed. The aim is to raise an interest in the change and provide a level of awareness of the intent of the change.

Coaches should consider communications that tell a story and depict what the future will look like following the change. One technique for this is distributing *postcards from the future*.

Postcards from the future

A postcard from the future is a vibrant picture from the near term future that shows what is possible. In essence, it is a picture of the vision.

To create a postcard from the future, coaches put themselves in the future looking back, not in the present looking forward. The picture should excite and motivate people to find out more. Coaches should not do it in isolation. They should do it in a workshop environment with members of the project team, key stakeholders, and other members of the change-coaching network.

The postcard should tell a compelling message and be somewhat futuristic but also be practical enough that is can be seen as achievable over a given period.

Imagine a global organization that couldn't collaborate effectively and, therefore, silos grew across the globe resulting in inconsistent processes and duplication of effort. Everyone in the organization was aware that this was an issue and a burning platform. As a result, a project was established to deliver a collaboration platform across all the offices around the globe.

It is important to note that stakeholders may be made up of very different groups with different needs. Therefore, one postcard may not resonate with everyone. So, a little more analysis of the stakeholders may be needed before postcard(s) are sent. They could be distributed electronically or physical via a desk drop. The latter can have a greater impact, as it is more tactile and personal.

ONE TEAM
No More Silos Anymore!

Wish you were here?

Project Collaboration
https://pcollaboration.com

Imperative

Depending on the nature and size of the change, an initial communication of intent may need to be sent via a senior executive within the organization to people managers so that they are furnished with the information required to have meaningful conversations with their teams. Coaches will facilitate this with assistance from the change managers as needed.

This could be supported by an information pack including details of where additional materials can be sourced.

This pack could describe the vision of the future and why the change is an imperative for the organization, and it should generate a sense of urgency. It should be written in a personable manner from the senior executive. It should include the who, what, where, and when of the change as best known.

Start the conversation

If a collaboration platform is available, coaches should establish communities in relation to the project. This will allow for conversation and collaboration. I say communities in the plural as coaches may have a community for change coaches, and one for the impacted stakeholders.

The conversation should be closely monitored as it will inform in regards to stakeholder needs and concerns, burning topics, and the appetite for more information.

If coaches don't have a collaboration platform, they can utilize collaboration areas, which were mentioned earlier. They can put up posters, drop postcards from the future, but always ensure they provide means by which everyone can seek out more information.

One way to garner a sense of what people want to know is to provide a question wall. This is an area upon which they can post sticky notes with a question. This is anonymous to encourage participation. Others can see what their colleagues are asking, which can prompt them to ask a different question.

Coaches can collate the questions into themes, and provide answers and feedback.

Communication effectiveness

It is important that the coaches constantly measure the success of the communication. One way to get an indication of the success of the communication is by looking at the data.

The data can tell coaches who is opening an email or clicking on a link. The following example is from my website, which tells me who is visiting my website. If I were communicating with the intent of engaging with both USA and India, the data tells me that my communication is not working with the Indian region.

Source: www.karenferris.com

Coaches can also use the same approach to test communications. Coaches can create two version of the same communication—A and B. Distribute A and B to two test groups of around 30 people in each and see what communication gets opened or clicked through. The one with the best reaction is the one that gets used.

Backlog analysis

Before coaches can start to think about a change plan or determine stakeholders' position in regards to the change, they need to take a look at the product backlog.

The product backlog is simply a list of all the things that need to be done within the project.

Once the initial product backlog has been groomed, activities for the sprints will be in a prioritized order based on business needs. Remember that the backlog gets groomed on a regular basis so an analysis will also be an ongoing activity.

When grooming takes place:

- User stories that are no longer relevant will be removed.
- New user stories will be added.
- Stories will be prioritized.
- Estimates (time, effort, and cost) will be assigned to stories that don't have one
- Existing estimates may get revised based on new information.
- User stories that appear too large to be completed within a sprint will be split into smaller stories.

Coaches should be actively involved in the backlog grooming and asking questions to ensure understanding of why particular actions are being taken.

As mentioned earlier, user stories are short, simple descriptions of a feature told from the perspective of the person who desires the new capability, usually a user or customer of the system. They typically follow a simple template:

As a < type of user >, I want < some goal > so that <some reason>.

For example:

As a <u>bank teller</u>, I want <u>to see the customer's debt when viewing an account balance</u>, so that <u>I can offer additional services to help manage the debt</u>.

So, the initial analysis will include determination of key stakeholders. The user stories inform coaches of the 'roles' requesting change. They are prioritized so coaches know which changes are likely to be in the next sprint.

Change on a page

During kick-off, coaches can start to put together the change plan-on-a-page based on what they know. Remember once again, that it will be a work in progress and possibly only 80% accurate at any given point. It is a fluid, flexible, and highly visible document to generate conversation and subsequent revision or validation.

This is the plan, as of the current time, regarding communications, engagement, alliances (i.e. the groups and social networks to be assembled, created and/or leveraged), training, and any other relevant activities that need to take place.

The following is an example of a plan-on-a-page. It should be at least A3, highly visible, and in a high traffic area. It should also be available online via the chosen collaboration platforms and tools.

A change plan-on-a-page could look like this.

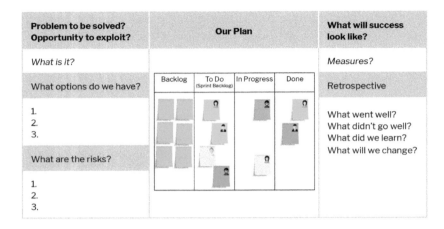

Change Plan-on-a-Page (inspired by Jason Little http://leanchange.org)

Baseline stakeholder position

Identification of stakeholders is an ongoing process. However, during kick-off, coaches will try to determine as many stakeholders as possible and their position in relation to the change. The purpose of baselining is to determine current stakeholder position, which will inform communication and engagement strategies.

	Time block 0	Time block 1	Time block 2	Time block 3	Time block 4	Time block 5
Comunication	Kick-off Message from CEO to people leaders Jive Information pack Start FAQ	Awareness Intranet articles Why - dd/mm/yyyy What - dd/mm/yyyy When - dd/mm/yyyy Who - - dd/mm/yyyy Infographic for employee lounges		Readiness Jive Q&A with CEO Q&A with super users Intranet articles	Go Live Postcards from the future 'Are you ready to rumble?' Support is here	Celebration Early adopters Good news stories Reinforcement comms
Engagement (using change coach network)	Engage ID change coaches needed Information pack Establish exchange	Inform 1 Q&A sessions with program lead	Inform 2 Information pack Video pack	Coach Change coaches informed and enabled to lead local engagement Readiness checks Remediation		Adoption Coaches check on adoption and undertake remediation action
Alliances	Establish Jive project group Jive people group ID Super use	ID Team meetings User forums Town halls Engage super users	Unite Coalition though identified forums Prototype & sandpit for super users	Information flow Continual engagement with alliances and provision of information		Check In Check in with alliances
Training	ID Identify trainers	Fundamentals July 31 - 2 August - Melbourne June 5 - 7 Sydney	Train the Trainer dd/mm/yyyy dd/mm/yyyy dd/mm/yyyy dd/mm/yyyy	Just in time training dd/mm/yyyy dd/mm/yyyy dd/mm/yyyy dd/mm/yyyy	Self Service Launch self service training portal Embed into on boarding process	
Other						

Traditionally, stakeholder position was tracked along a change curve. The change curve is based on the grief cycle introduced by Swiss-American psychiatrist, Elisabeth Kubler-Ross in her 1969 book *On Death and Dying*. The grief cycle was meant to reflect how people coped with illness and dying.

The five stages of grief (denial, anger, bargaining, depression, and acceptance) have also been used to describe how people react to significant changes in the workplace.

The *Change Curve* shown below also indicates the activities coaches can utilize to move people from one stage to the next.

The overall aim is to move everyone along the curve as quickly as possible to the point of acceptance.

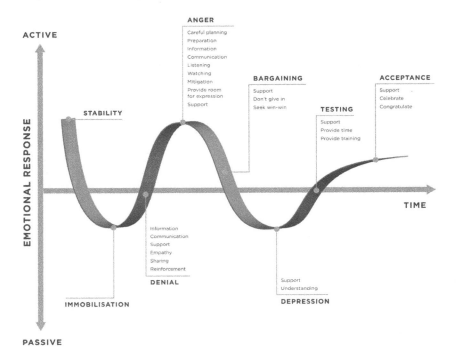

The change curve still serves a purpose in understanding how people may transition through change. It should also be noted, that later in her life Kubler-Ross regretted writing the stages in a linear manner as she recognized they were not as linear and predictable as the model appeared to illustrate.

While it is useful to know where people are on their change journey, coaches may not have the time or resources to undertake the research and analysis across all stakeholder groups and put in place tactics to move people along the curve when change is rapid and constant.

Coaches might have to be much more subjective and utilise tools such as the Change Scorecard. The aim is to determine the tools that are fit-for-purpose, best suited to determine where stakeholders are currently at, and create a baseline.

Social networks

A good way to baseline stakeholder position is to tap into the various social networks within the organization. In a truly agile organization, there may be squads, chapters, tribes, and guilds that coaches can reach out to assist with baselining.

These structures have ceremonies including daily stand-ups, sprint planning, retrospectives, and iteration reviews. All of these can provide a sense of stakeholder position.

At the core of the agile way of working is the concept of continual feedback loops. Feedback loops are the mechanism used to validate that the progress being made meets business needs and obtains both positive and negative feedback that can be fed into process improvement. These feedback loops are an intrinsic part of the agile ceremonies.

Social networks also include the communication and collaboration platforms within an organization. Listening and watching the conversations taking place can also provide a feeling about stakeholder position.

These social networks are where our network of change coaches need to become embedded so they can determine stakeholder position and inform the ongoing communication and engagement approaches.

ADKAR®

ADKAR® is a model from Prosci.[1] Created by Jeff Hiatt, ADKAR® is an acronym that represents five outcomes an individual must achieve for change to be successful. The outcomes are awareness, desire, knowledge, ability, and reinforcement®.

The purpose of ADKAR® is to assist organizational change management identify where a person or team is in regards to the change journey and then put in place strategies to move them through subsequent steps of the model.

My purpose is not to describe the ADKAR® model and its various applications in detail. That information can be ascertained from the Prosci website and supporting publications.

However, the following table provides a high-level description of each ADKAR® step and some of the strategies coaches can put in place to move people through each step of the model.

ADKAR® MODEL		
Step	Explanation	Strategies
Awareness	Awareness of the business need for the change and the implications of not changing.	Communication Coaching Active change coaches
Desire	Desire to engage and participate in the change.	Communication Coaching Active change coaches Support
Knowledge	Knowledge about how to change.	Communication Coaching Education Training

Ability	Ability to realise or implement the change and perform at the level required.	Communication
		Coaching
		Active change coaches
		Hands-on training
		Train-the-trainer
		Super-users
Reinforcement	Reinforcement to ensure the change sticks.	Communication
		Coaching
		Active change coaches
		Measure and monitor
		Corrective action
		Celebrations

Coaches could use the ADKAR® steps on a Change Scorecard, and then get the assistance of the change-coaching network to determine where each stakeholder group is on the model and reflect the position with a traffic light indicator. This would form the baseline.

Change managers can then support the change coaches, and provide assistance with strategies to move the stakeholder groups along the model.

Progress along the model can be shown via the traffic light indicators.

Lean Coffee

Lean Coffee is a great way to determine where stakeholders are at and provides a regular check-in on their position. Change coaches can hold Lean Coffee sessions in their local area. The invitation to Lean Coffee does not specify what is to be discussed.

Lean Coffee is a structured meeting but has no agenda. The idea was started in Seattle in 2009 with the aim of creating a fluid and dynamic group that would discuss lean techniques but without the structure of steering groups, committees, speakers, agendas etc. The initiators, Jim Benson and Jeremy Lightsmith, just wanted people who wanted to learn and share, to turn up.

This is how it works.

1. Coaches create a Kanban board with three columns: to discuss, discussing, discussed.

2. They provide everyone with sticky notes and a pen. People write down what they want to discuss and put the sticky note in the first column—to discuss. They include their name in case they need to provide clarity on the topic.

3. When there is a critical mass, the change coach spends a few minutes introducing each topic, sharing a sentence or two describing the idea on each sticky note.

4. Each person then gets three votes. Using sticky dots, they cast their vote on the sticky note they wish to discuss. They can spread their three votes across two or three sticky notes or place them all on one sticky note.

5. The sticky notes with the most votes are moved to the top of the 'to discuss' column in order of popularity.

6. Coaches now have an agenda. Depending on the time allowed for the session, coaches may only discuss one topic or they may discuss more. Coaches move the sticky notes they think can be discussed into the 'discussing' column.

7. Each topic has a time limit. This could be five or ten minutes. The group can agree on a time box.

8. When the time is reached, the group votes on continuing the discussion or moving on to the next topic. Voting is a

simple roman vote: thumbs up, down or sideways. This makes it easy to see what the group wants to do.

9. If discussion is to continue, coaches can reduce the time box and continue the discussion. This step can be repeated as many times as necessary until the group indicates it's wish to move on to another topic.

10. When the group wants to move on, coaches move the topic into the 'discussed' column and bring over the next highest sticky note from 'to be discussed' into the 'discussing' column.

11. Coaches repeat the process.

12. At the end of the session, coaches elicit feedback from the group. They can capture the Kanban board by taking a photo for future reference.

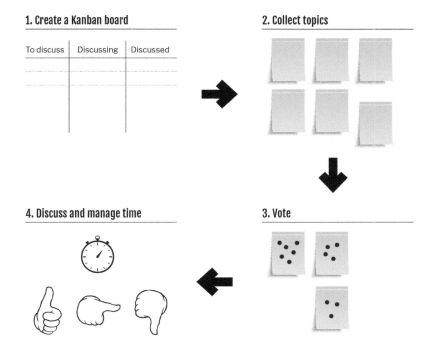

1. Create a Kanban board

To discuss	Discussing	Discussed

2. Collect topics

4. Discuss and manage time

3. Vote

Lean Coffee Process

Lean Coffee will inform coaches about what the stakeholders want to know or are concerned about. The attendees at a Lean Coffee session will also indicate the cohort(s) who want to know more. Those who don't attend could also indicate disengagement and warrant further investigation to determine what communication and engagement strategies are needed.

Because the attendees set the agenda, they have a vested interest and buy-in. Therefore, Lean Coffee is also a means of increasing engagement.

Remember that Lean Coffee can be used for meetings when we want to have an open-ended conversation that is owned and directed by the attendees, and when we want to discuss what the attendees see as a priority up front. Lean Coffee can be used for team meetings, ideation, and retrospectives.

Once again, there are online tools for Lean Coffee if there are constraints in getting people in the same locality. These include Retrium, Instant Agenda, and Lean Coffee Table.

Personas

A quick way to determine position in relation to the change is to develop personas. Personas are developed as part of user experience (UX) design and may already have been developed as part of the project. If they already exist, the change coaches can leverage them. If they don't exist, the change coaches can develop them.

Personas are fictional characters that represent the different consumer types that might use a service, product, site or brand in a similar way. They are typically used to describe external stakeholder groups but coaches can also use them to describe internal stakeholder groups.

Personas help us understand stakeholder needs, experiences, and goals. They aid the recognition that different people have different needs and expectations. Not only does it feed the design process but it can also aid change coaches in providing a human touch and understanding what makes people tick.

Creating personas help us determine stakeholder groups that might require customized attention. It can inform communication content and approaches as well as engagement practices and training needs.

Personas can be ratified as change progresses, shared with the coaching network, and reused for future changes.

Ordinate amount of time could be spent on creating personas but we don't have that time. A few quick lean personas are better than nothing at all. Lean personas tend to be built from qualitative data rather than quantitative. The latter takes longer to collect and interpret. The approach will depend on the nature of the change. Steps could include:

1. Online research: For example, research personas by using Google to gather information about age groups, demographics, roles, occupations etc.

2. Validation with the coaching network: Build some quick personas based on what is known and then validate with other coaches that match the profile.

3. Quick interviews: Conduct interviews with stakeholders. The minimum for fairly accurate results is five. The common range is 5–30 and the number will be determined by the time available.

The following are sample questions that could be asked. The questions used will need to reflect what coaches want to learn about the stakeholders/players.

Coach: When you go to the procurement application, what are your goals?

Player 1: I want to get bargains and save as much money as I can.

Player 2: I want to get in and out as fast as I can. I hate procurement.

Player 3: I want the newest technology and apps available.

Coach: When you go to *My Online Portal* to review your education and training, what are your goals?

Player 1: I want just one click to see my history.

Player 2: I want to have clarity of outstanding training.

Player 3: I want to see the training by the required completion date on one page so I can decide what to do next.

When creating the personas include the following:

Name and photo: Coaches can give them a nickname based on their behavior such as *Cool Dude*

Roles: Surveys can be useful to capture this information. If there are a large number of 'business analysts' create a 'business analyst' specific persona. Include the role and department.

Goals and needs: Why do they make their decisions? What are their fears? What are their goals?

Behaviors and beliefs: What are their characteristics?

Personality: Are they introvert or extrovert?

When coaches have enough to establish categories of attribution, i.e. commonalities between stakeholders, the stakeholder can then be plotted and similar people combined into a persona. In the example below, Steve could be a combination of two other real people with the same characteristics of technical ability and social media presence.

Name: Steve

'Proto' Persona: Cool Dude

Bio

- Age: 27
- Education: Undergraduate
- Role: Graphic designer
- Department: UX
- Tenure: 1.5 years
- Location: Melbourne
- Direct reports: 0
- Indirect reports: 2

Behaviors & Beliefs

- Will do whatever it takes to get ahead
- Works long hours including weekends
- Values efficiency - will use any tools that get the job done quicker
- Great socializer - makes business contacts in social environments
- Confident and unstoppable
- Uses social media channels actively including Twitter, Facebook and Instagram
- Self starter

Personality

Introvert	———●———	Extrovert
Judging	——●———	Feeling
Thinking	———●——	Perceiving
Sensing	———●——	Intuition

Goals and Needs

- Tools that are easy to use
- Tools that speed up the job
- Leading edge technology to do the job
- Knowledge hungry
- Industry expert
- The go-to person
- Frustrated with the hierarchies and bureaucracies in business that slow everything down

Technology

Internet	———————●—
Software	——●—————
Mobile apps	————●———

The change coach network can create personas that represent the various segments of the organization, which can be utilized on various change initiatives. The key is not to assume that the personas are static. Personas can change over time and, therefore, require maintenance.

Empathy map

When we have our personas, we can build an empathy map for a particular scenario, product, or service.

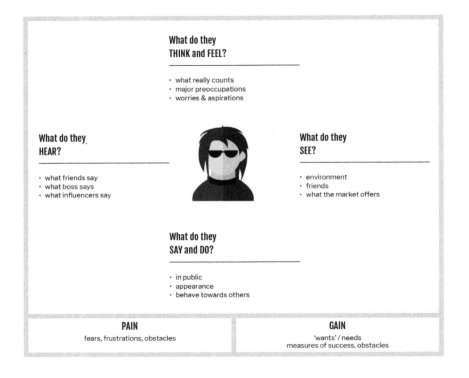

Coaches, along with their colleagues should spend a few minutes reflecting on a persona. The thoughts should be captured in each of the four quadrants of the *Empathy Map* as shown above.

What they are SEEING?

What are they seeing in their environment? What is happening with their friends or colleagues (that they are seeing)? What else is changing that they are seeing? What other experiences or product alternatives are they seeing outside the organization that relate to this change?

What do they THINK and FEEL?

What might they be thinking? What might they believe? What are they preoccupied by? What are their potential worries or aspirations? What really matters or counts to them? What are their personal priorities? What emotions might they be feeling?

What do they HEAR?

What are they hearing inside and outside the organization? What rumors might they be hearing? What are their colleagues saying about this change? What are their peers, in other departments, saying about this change?

What might they SAY or DO?

What defining statements has the persona said (or might say)? What actions or behaviors have been noticed (or are being envisioned in that persona)? What is their attitude in public? What is their appearance? What is their behavior toward others?

What is their PAIN?

What are some of their potential pain points or fears as it relates to the change? What might hold them back from supporting the change? What will this change remove?

What is their GAIN?

What might they gain or benefit from this change? What's in it for them if they support the change? Why do they (or should they) want to adopt a new way of working?

Force field analysis

Force field analysis is a method to determine the driving forces for change and the restraining forces. The driving forces have to be stronger than the restraining forces in order to upset the status quo and make the change happen.

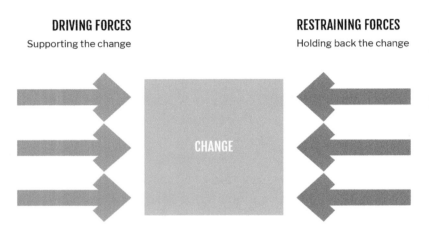

In the diagram above, the *driving forces* are equal to the restraining forces, so the status quo will not be disrupted.

The lean community also refers to Force Field Analysis as Perspectives Mapping.

The perceived forces for and against a change can be gathered from various groups of stakeholders. This allows different perspectives to be surfaced and common views identified.

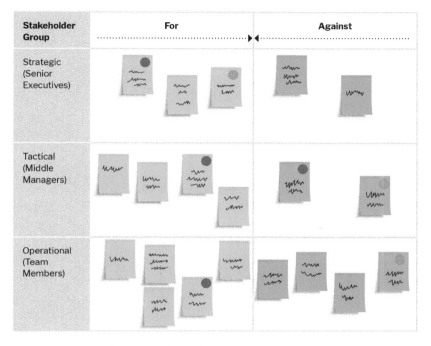

Stakeholder Group	For			Against		
Strategic (Senior Executives)						
Tactical (Middle Managers)						
Operational (Team Members)						

● Common Perspective 1
● Common Perspective 2

Perspectives Mapping (inspired by Jason Little http://leanchange.org)

The stakeholders could be the business and technology to determine if there are different perspectives in relation to a change. The stakeholders could be strategic, tactical, and operational i.e. senior executives, middle management, and team members.

In a safe environment, coaches can give one of the stakeholder groups a sheet of butcher's paper. They draw a line down the middle and on the left hand side write FOR and on the right hand side they write AGAINST. Then, using sticky notes they identify things *for* and *against* a particular change.

The facilitator, usually a change coach, discusses the results to gain further insights as necessary. The process is then repeated with the other groups.

The coach will then analyze the outputs from each group and look for common perspectives and where perspectives differ between the groups. This can then inform decision-making about how to align the groups and how to increase the drivers for change if the restraining forces are greater.

Coaches can also add a further level of granularity and ask about the *for* and *against* perspectives related to particular aspects of the change e.g. process, people, communication, engagement etc.

In light of transparency, the results from all stakeholder groups and the common perspectives should be shared with all stakeholder groups and discussed.

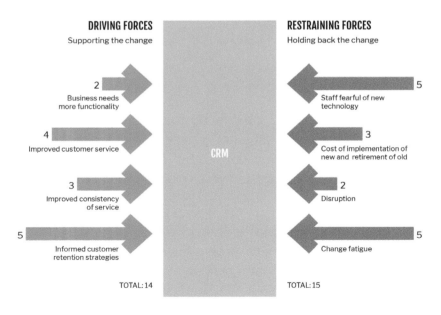

Force field analysis can be taken a step further if needed. The driving forces for change and the restraining forces can be weighted.

In the example opposite, each of the forces driving the change or restraining the change have been weighted by the stakeholder groups and the weightings averaged out across all groups. The averaged weightings would then be reviewed and agreed with all stakeholder groups.

Once agreed, decisions can be made as to how to increase the total score of the driving forces and/or decrease the total score of the restraining forces so that the score on the left is relatively higher than that on the right.

Baseline

Once coaches have determined stakeholder position in relation to the change, they can capture the baseline on the change scorecard.

Coaches can add a row to the change scorecard that shows overall position (baseline). This can be updated as stakeholder position changes. In the example below, I have used smiley faces to indicate stakeholder position: happy, neutral, unhappy. This provides an instant picture of progress.

Measures	Region 1	Region 2	Region 3	Region 4
STAKEHOLDER POSITION	☹	☺	😐	☺
Awareness	●	●	●	●
Understanding	●	●	●	●
Training	●	●	●	●
Knowledge	●	●	●	●
Coaches	●	●	●	●
Leadership	●	●	●	●
Ability	●	●	●	●
Active collaboration	●	●	●	●

● Not started
● Uh-oh!
● Close
● Excellent

Kit bags

On agile delivery, change coaches need to be thinking more than just one sprint ahead. Aware that the direction of the project may chop and change based on changing business priorities or feedback received, the coaches (with the support of change managers) have to do more preparation on agile projects than on waterfall projects.

On waterfall projects, the outcomes, stakeholders, delivery dates, etc. were all well known before the project commenced and, therefore, the change team knew exactly what to prepare for. On agile projects, coaches are not really sure what they have to prepare for. They do not have the level of certainly that waterfall delivery offers.

As a result, the coaches have to create what I call *kit bags*. These kit bags address the 'what if' scenarios. They contain upfront preparation that can be pulled out depending on where the project is at and where it is going.

Let's say the coaches know that a stakeholder group is the marketing team. They are not sure when they will be impacted. The kit bag they create is the engagement and communication approach for marketing based on what they know about them at this time. They may know how they would like to be engaged and the sort of messaging that will resound with them.

So, coaches can prepare a kit bag for marketing engagement and communication with as much information as they have now. They cannot wait until sprint planning and realize they thought this sprint would impact the graphic design team but actually it's now going to impact marketing.

This is where coaches pull out the appropriate kit bag, add in the missing detail, and utilize it.

Of course coaches already have a kit bag for the graphic design team, which they are not going to utilize on this sprint but they may on the next.

Kit bags mean coaches are as *best prepared as they can be* to respond to the uncertainty that can often be agile delivery. The kit bags can be labeled with the names of known stakeholder groups. They can contain communication and engagement approaches (the means by which stakeholder readiness will be assessed), training approaches, and the means to monitor and measure progress.

Coaches may wish to do the opposite and label the kit bags with the names of organizational change activities such as communications, engagement, training etc. and have the approaches for each stakeholder group within each kit bag.

Kit bags mean coaches are equipped and organized.

Outputs

Some of the outputs from this stage may include:

- Change on a page
- Lean Coffee sessions
- Personas
- Empathy maps
- Force field analysis
- Perspective mapping
- Change scorecard with stakeholder baseline position
- Kit bags.

Sprints

In this stage, coaches continue the development and deployment of their communication and engagement activities. Coaches put in place measures to determine progress and inform any remediation action required. Coaches continue to analyze the backlog and look at the user stories. Stakeholder assessment and readiness is performed, progress is monitored, and the build of training commences.

Coaches continue to use the tools previously described, as needed e.g. Kanban boards, change scorecards, Lean Coffee, story-telling etc.

Communication and engagement

The key role of the coach during this stage is to maintain continual communication and engagement with the stakeholders and the players impacted by the outcome of the sprint(s).

The communication and engagement techniques can continue to be deployed.

Regular checks should be made to ensure that communication and engagement is having the desired effect. There should be systematic check-ins with stakeholders to ascertain whether the messages were received and understood. If they are not, the communication and engagement approaches will have to be changed or refined.

A significant objective of communication and engagement is to garner involvement of the players. The players are the ones who have to adjust to the changed playing conditions and, therefore, have to be the co-creators of the future state.

The coaches not only need to communicate and engage the players on the journey but also train and prepare them along the way.

Commitment

One of the activities that the coach needs to undertake during sprint planning is commitment from people to deliver what is asked of them. A commitment canvas can be used for this.

A commitment canvas provides clarity about who is accountable for making things happen. It captures the who, what, where, and when. It should be displayed in a highly visible area (either physically or virtually). Ideally, it contains a picture or avatar of the person accountable for the action and their signature as a commitment to deliver.

The following is an example of a *Commitment Canvas*.

Who	What	When	Comment	Signed
	Update the web site	Every Monday morning	Will shift forward when there are public holidays	*Ken*
	Facilitate Lean Coffee sessions	At least one per sprint		*Bill*
	I will provide Ken with the content for the website	Every Friday afternoon	Will shift forward when there are public holidays	*Sally*
	Deliver working software	Every increment	Primary measure of success	*Keith*
	Remove obstacles	As needed		*John*
	Deliver working software	Every increment	Primary measure of success	*Helen*

Metaphors

During communication, consider the use of metaphors. Metaphors are more effective than text vision or goal statements. A metaphor is a visual representation of the end-goal. It should spark conversation and can generate valuable feedback.

The following is an example of a metaphor intended to explain the role of organizational change management when change is constant.

When change is volatile, uncertain, complex and ambiguous

Organizational change management guides us safely on the journey

Backlog analysis and user stories

The content of communication and nature of engagement will be informed by analysis of the sprint backlog.

The sprint backlog is a list of tasks identified by the project team to be completed during the next sprint. During a sprint-planning meeting, the project team will select a number of product backlog items (usually in the form of user stories) and identify the tasks necessary to complete each user story. The effort required to complete each task will be estimated so that there is confidence that the sprint backlog chosen can be completed within the allocate sprint duration.

Let's take a closer look at what we can ascertain from user stories to inform impact assessment. We can leverage user stories to tell us who, what, why, and how. The following is a user story example.

'As a recruitment officer, I want to complete an expedited offer by which the candidate and public service agency are simultaneously informed and the candidate response evaluated to ensure all required documentation has been provided to meet regulatory requirements.'

This user story tells us the following:

WHO: recruitment officer.

WHAT: complete an expedited offer by which the candidate and public service agency are simultaneously informed and the candidate response evaluated to ensure all required documentation has been provided.

WHY: to meet regulatory requirements.

It also tells us that there are actually four stakeholders in this user story.

The key stakeholder is the recruitment officer. The other stakeholders are the candidate, the public service agency, and the person or team observing regulatory conformance in the recruitment process.

The user story also provides us with a scenario. The recruitment officer needs to complete an *expedited offer*; this scenario will need to be included in the training.

This is a great start for change coaches to determine stakeholder, impact, and readiness.

Stakeholder impact assessment

They key thing to remember is that we are replacing the heavyweight stakeholder impact and readiness assessments with a lightweight means of assessing the impacts of sprints quickly and through conversations. As mentioned earlier, coaches can leverage the wider change coach network and call on them to assist with sizing.

Impact assessment might be as simple as using t-shirt sizing to indicate a small, medium, large, or extra large impact.

Impact assessment will be conducted sprint-by-sprint.

Utilizing the user stories, coaches can determine (for each sprint) whether the impact is on the same stakeholders or new stakeholders.

At the end of the sprint, the coach or coaches can observe the product demonstrations that will be conducted with the stakeholders (players) and look for the ah-ha moments where a visual presentation in a particular context can surface impacts that had not been considered earlier and can now be incorporated in the readiness tasks.

As impact assessments are being conducted sprint-by-sprint, the change coaches will be updating the blast radius as more information becomes available.

Additional impacted groups may be added, moved, or removed as additional clarity is acquired.

In the following example, a new stakeholder group (*legal*) has been added to the blast radius. Indicators have also been added to illustrate the stakeholder groups that are being impacted by the current sprint—sprint 2.

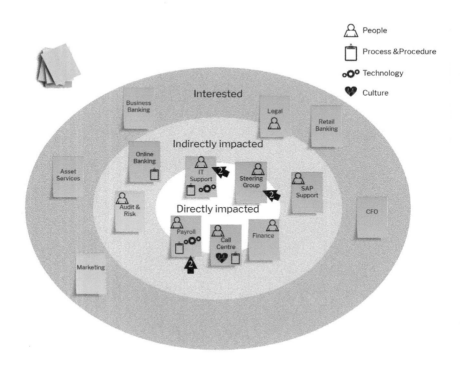

Updated blast radius by sprint (inspired by Jason Little
https://leanchange.org/resources/blastradius/)

Stakeholder readiness

During every sprint, coaches can determine stakeholder readiness by utilizing tools including social networks, ADKAR®, and Lean Coffee. The change scorecard can be updated as readiness is assessed.

Coaches can use the change scorecard with ADKAR®. Each of the ADKAR® steps can be placed in the 'measures' column and stakeholder position in relation to each step plotted using colored sticky dots.

See the example *Change Scorecard* using the *ADKAR®* model below.

Measures	Region 1	Region 2	Region 3	Region 4
STAKEHOLDER POSITION	☺	☺	☺	☺
Awareness	●	●	●	●
Desire	●	●	●	●
Knowledge	●	●	●	●
Ability	●	●	●	●
Reinforcement	●	●	●	●

● Not started
● Uh-oh!
○ Close
● Excellent

Monitor and measure

Coaches must continually monitor and measure stakeholder readiness. There are two measurements that can be used—qualitative and quantitative.

Qualitative measures

Qualitative data can be gathered via interviews and methods such as Lean Coffee and listening into social networks. The data will be subjective but we can plot the data to allow progress to be measured. We can determine the readiness of heart, mind, and body and create a readiness monitor.

Readiness of **heart** is indicated by enthusiasm for a change, acknowledging the uncertainly when change is constant, and positive talking.

Readiness of **mind** is indicated by curiosity and asking pertinent questions about the change. It is demonstrated when people seek out more information and share that information with colleagues.

Readiness of **body** is demonstrated when people get actively involved in activities related to the change. This could include offering to be a trainer, assist with communications or volunteering to become a change coach.

Each of these can be measured along a continuum and progress along the continuum monitored. This measure is subjective but it is an indicator and can be ratified with other change coaches and colleagues.

The following is an example of how this readiness could be illustrated and tracked.

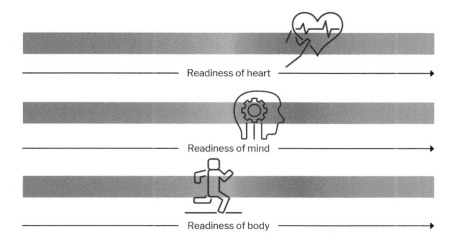

Readiness of heart

Readiness of mind

Readiness of body

Quantitative measures

Quantitative measures include surveys or pulse checks. In a rapidly changing environment, if surveys are deployed they have to be simple, fast, and easy to complete. Wherever possible, the results should be automatically computed. Speed is of the essence when deploying surveys.

Surveys should be used with caution. If coaches survey for every change, very quickly there will be survey fatigue and returns will quickly diminish. Therefore, choose carefully the changes for which surveys are utilized.

The changes should be critical, where quantitative data will provide significant value in ensuring desired outcomes are achieved. The change could be widespread with a large number of stakeholder groups and, therefore, subjective assessment of change readiness is considered a risk. In all other cases, subjective data will have to be good enough.

One option is to deploy the ADKAR® self-assessment survey and then analyze the returns.

I would try and make this process even faster by turning it into a pulse check. Using the intranet, collaboration platform, or mobile application (preferred) ask one question with five options (following the ADKAR® model) and provide space for questions or feedback. If using a mobile application, the survey can be pushed out and responses automatically collated.

The five questions could look something like this. Note I have deliberately avoided the term 'survey'.

PROJECT ABC CANVASS	
We are interested in your views on this change. Please choose from one of the options below.	
1. I am aware of this change and its purpose	☐
2. I have the desire to undertake this change	☐
3. I believe I have the knowledge to undertake this change	☐
4. I believe I have the ability to undertake this change	☐
5. None of the above	☐
Please leave comments here.	

Build training

Training on agile delivery is built as the sprints progress. The training will be delivered in the 'strike' phase (also known as release).

Training on agile projects is quite different to that on waterfall projects. On waterfall projects, the players (the end-users) get product updates in large batches. On agile projects, updates are more frequent and smaller; therefore, end-users have less to learn.

Also, on agile projects, collaboration across all stakeholder groups including the end-user is paramount. The end-users are far more familiar with what is being delivered due to their involvement. This makes these end-users ideal trainers who can train the rest of the end-users.

At the end of a sprint, there is a sprint review. The product is presented to the stakeholders (including end-users) usually in the format of a demonstration. This is a hands-on approach so that feedback can be provided to the project team. The feedback could mean that changes are required or that we now have a shippable product.

In other words, the sprint review equates to a form of end-user training. In many cases, this level of training may be sufficient for these end-users to train others. In other cases, some train-the-trainer activities may be required to bolster the end-user training and equip these 'super-users' to train others.

The availability of help files, supporting documentation, frequently asked questions and answers, online assistance, quick reference guides, presentations, and videos etc. will support the training and will be built sprint-by-sprint. The production of these artefacts will be included in the 'definition of done' which is agreed at the start of every sprint.

The people developing this content become skilled training developers who are immersed in their content and this will be important during the final stages of testing when last minutes changes are identified, and quick and effective updates to training materials are required.

Training content is built using the user-stories (the who, what, and why). Content also comes from the feedback from the product demonstrations, the final code in the test environment, and any feedback earmarked as a future enhancement.

Outputs

Some of the outputs from this stage may include:

- Metaphors
- Blast radius
- Change scorecard
- Quantitative and qualitative data
- Readiness monitor
- Pulse check
- Training built.

CHAPTER 39

Strike

This is the penultimate stage before a shippable product is delivered.

Communication and engagement

The coach will maintain continual communication and engagement with the stakeholders and the players impacted by delivery of the shippable product.

The regular checks made during the sprints to ensure that the communication and engagement approaches were having the desired effect should give us comfort that the approach being used at this stage is the right one.

Monitor and measure

Coaches must continue to measure stakeholder readiness for the change right up to the point of go-live.

Training

Training will be delivered during the strike (release) phase prior to go-live. During this period, the training materials will be finalized, trainers identified and trained, training site(s) prepared, and training conducted.

Depending on the nature of the training, users may need to be scheduled to attend training. This may entail logistics in the provision of physical or virtual classrooms.

Wherever possible, instructor-led hands-on training should be utilized. This reduces the need for extensive training materials as the training is undertaken using the systems being delivered. Quick reference guides may be provided but computer based training (CBT) videos and reams of documentation are not required. CBT may be created once the systems have been stabilized. If it is created before that point, it will have to be continually updated as last minute changes are made.

Hands-on training also allows last minute changes to be made when training uncovers something that is not working as expected.

Feedback will be obtained throughout the initial training delivery and through subsequent use of training materials and updates incorporated in order to continually improve the training experience.

Super-users

The end-users who took part in the user acceptance testing or end-user testing (also referred to as beta users) should be engaged during training. They are the super-users, the subject-matter experts and will make ideal facilitators if not trainers.

Wherever possible they should have participated in train-the-trainer activities and be ready and equipped to deliver the training in this stage as needed. As training is delivered, they will be able to provide feedback on the training materials so that improvements can be made.

They should also be deployed as floorwalkers at go-live. This means they are on hand at the physical location where the change is deployed if assistance and support is needed.

Outputs

Some of the outputs from this stage may include:

* Change scorecard

* Quantitative and qualitative data

* Training delivered.

CHAPTER 40

Score

This is where the business feels the value. This is where the goals are scored.

Communication and engagement

Upon go-live, coaches will continue to communicate and engage. They will support the existing users and revert to the sprint-by-sprint tasks for the next iteration.

Coaches will communicate the results of go-live and share success stories and lessons learnt.

Communications will contain celebrations, acknowledgments, and rewards.

As the sprints wrap up and the systems stabilize, the communication may only be in relation to updates to the systems to provide minor fixes and enhancements.

Monitor and measure

User adoption will be monitored and measured to determine if any post go-live organizational change management activities are needed. With all the work that has taken place in the previous stages, and the active involvement and ownership of the change by the players, post go-live remediation activities should be minor in nature.

Review and retrospective

A retrospective is a meeting held at the end of each iteration. It reviews what went well, what could be improved, and the next steps. In simple terms, it asks the team three questions.

What are we going to start doing?
What are we going to stop doing?
What are we going to continue doing?

The project will be conducting a retrospective, and I suggest that the coach and any change management colleagues involved with the project take part in this retrospective rather than have a standalone one. Lessons learnt on all aspects of the project can then be shared openly.

Determine ongoing support requirements

Ongoing support requirements may include the conversion of training to CBT. This can then be made available as part of on boarding and training for new or transferred employees. It can also be made available as refresher training when needed.

Feedback from the players will inform the coaches of any other ongoing support requirements.

PART 10

BRINGING IT HOME

CHAPTER 41

A game played well

Unlike in the world of soccer, organizations do not have the luxury of extra time in which they can hope and dream that they can score a last minute goal and beat the opposition.

Organizations have to act <u>now</u> and build a winning team that is resilient in the face of constant change.

Every soccer team needs a group of players with complementary skills that make a great team. It is the same in a winning organization. It needs skilled, capable and resilient players, great change coaches and formidable change managers.

The team needs continual development to maintain and sustain its resilience to constant change.

The team needs good leadership. It is the team on the field that is critical but it is also the leadership on the sidelines that ensures they win the game.

Leadership brings it all together through collaboration, cohesion, and a shared sense of purpose.

Good leaders ensure that there is clarity of roles within the team and that the team plays to the strengths and capabilities of all the players.

There are continual feedback loops resulting in continual improvement. The team keeps going from strength to strength and adapting to ever changing conditions.

There is minimal (or no) hierarchy, absence of command and control, player autonomy, and a highly effective coalition of managers, coaches, and players.

It is these teams that score goals and win championships.

It is these organizations that achieve exceptional results and are leaders in their industry.

They bring it home. It's the beautiful game.

Endnotes

Chapter 1

1. https://www.imaworldwide.com/aim-change-management-methodology
2. https://www.prosci.com
3. https://www.managementexchange.com/blog/no-more-heroes
4. http://www.valvesoftware.com/company/Valve_Handbook_LowRes.pdf
5. https://www.ted.com/talks/ricardo_semler_how_to_run_a_company_with_almost_no_rules/transcript?language=en#t-369524
6. Formation describes how players are positioned on the pitch. For example, a 4-5-1 has four defenders, five midfielders, and one forward. Chelsea began its season with a 4-2-4 and changed, mid-season, to a 3-4-3. Conte had significant success with this formation at other clubs, which led him to adapt and switch formations.

Chapter 3

1. https://www.zappos.com/c/about-zappos-culture

Chapter 5

1. http://agilemanifesto.org

Chapter 6

1. https://www.gore.com/about/working-at-gore
2. http://www.self-managementinstitute.org/about/what-is-self-management

Chapter 7

1. http://morningstarco.com/index.cgi?Page=Self-Management

Chapter 8

1. http://mallenbaker.net/article/inspiring-people/ricardo-semler-the-radical-boss-who-proved-that-workplace-democracy-works

Chapter 9

1. https://www.cnet.com/news/what-ronaldinho-and-soccer-can-teach-you-about-innovation/

2. http://morningstarco.com/index.cgi?Page=About%20Us/Company%20History

3. https://www.gore.com/about/culture

4. http://www.goal.com/story/the-demise-of-dutch-football/index.html

Chapter 11

1. http://www.valvesoftware.com/company/Valve_Handbook_LowRes.pdf

Chapter 12

1. http://www.self-managementinstitute.org/about/what-is-self-management

Chapter 13

1. http://www.co2partners.com/how-to-flatten-a-hierarchy/

2. https://www.linkedin.com/pulse/neither-entitled-nor-titled-why-we-have-titles-gusto-jessica-yuen/

Chapter 14

1. http://www.supermarketnews.com/news/walmart-restructure-reduce-divisions-regions

2. https://www.canadianbusiness.com/innovation/how-flat-hierarchies-help-companies-stay-nimble-and-grow-faster/

Chapter 15

1. http://www.self-managementinstitute.org/about/what-is-self-management

2. https://www.managementexchange.com/blog/no-more-heroes

3. http://selfdeterminationtheory.org/

4. http://media.steampowered.com/apps/valve/Valve_NewEmployeeHandbook.pdf

5. http://www.valvesoftware.com/company/people.html

Chapter 16

1. http://fortune.com/best-companies/
2. https://www.gore.com/about/our-beliefs-and-principles
3. http://fortune.com/best-companies/fedex-corporation/

Chapter 17

1. http://wirearchy.com/what-is-wirearchy/

Chapter 20

1. http://missionandvalues.co/episodes/gumroad/

Chapter 21

1. https://www.gore.com/about/our-beliefs-and-principles

Chapter 22

1. http://morningstarco.com/index.cgi?Page=About Us%2FColleague
   Principles

Chapter 23

1. https://www.boeing.com/principles/employee-safety.page

Chapter 29

1. https://www.gore.com/about/working-at-gore
2. http://media.steampowered.com/apps/valve/Valve_Handbook_LowRes.
   pdf

Chapter 31

1. http://www.ritzcarlton.com/en/about/gold-standards
2. https://news.gallup.com/opinion/gallup/224012/dismal-employee-
   engagement-sign-global-mismanagement.aspx

Chapter 32

1. https://www.space.com/17547-jfk-moon-speech-50years-anniversary.
   html
2. https://www.aboutamazon.com/our-leadership-principles
3. http://fortune.com/change-the-world/2016/list
4. https://news.gallup.com/reports/199961/7.aspx
5. https://casper.com

Chapter 33

1. Formation describes how players are positioned on the pitch. For example, a 4-5-1 has four defenders, five midfielders, and one forward. Chelsea began its season with a 4-2-4 and changed, mid-season, to a 3-4-3. Conte had significant success with this formation at other clubs, which led him to adapt and switch formations.

Chapter 37

1. https://www.prosci.com/adkar/adkar-model

WORKING WITH KAREN

You can engage Karen in the following ways:

FACILITATOR (workshops)

- Three roles, and only three, for effective organizational change management
- Change resilience for individuals
- Change resilience for teams
- Change resilience for leaders
- Leaders who lead
- Leaders who let go
- Flattening the hierarchy
- Organizational change management at speed
- Change tools for an age of agility
- Adaptive leadership

TRAINER

Training courses are available for all levels of your organization, and based on any of the subjects facilitated at workshops.

SPEAKER

Keynote speaker for your next event based on any of the subjects facilitated at workshops. Keynotes are tailored to your needs and those of your organization or audience.

COACH

Coaching for teams and individuals who need to evolve in line with the evolution of the business.

Coaching for change practitioners needing to revise their approach to align with the speed of the organization.

Coaching for leaders who need to become more effective and adaptive.

MENTOR

Grow and learn through a mentoring relationship with Karen by sharing her wisdom and experience.

AUTHOR

Contributing thought-provoking content for your next publication.

CONNECTING WITH KAREN

Twitter: @karen_ferris

LinkedIn: https://www.linkedin.com/in/karenferris/

Facebook: https://www.facebook.com/
                    karenferristhoughtleaderOCM/

Instagram: karenferrisdotcom

∞

CPSIA information can be obtained
at www.ICGtesting.com
Printed in the USA
LVHW071502110919
630432LV00018B/248/P